# YOU, INC.

You Are
This Business

T~~~~

# YOU, INC.

## THE STEP BY STEP GUIDE FOR
## FINDING A BUSINESS WITHIN YOU

# TRAVIS ROSSER

**LIONCREST**
PUBLISHING

YOU, INC.
*The Step by Step Guide for Finding a Business Within You*

ISBN   978-1-5445-1164-1 *Paperback*
        978-1-5445-1163-4 *Ebook*

*To my two sons, Kyle and Conor. I hope they can look at me one day and know that despite my imperfections and my failures, I was able to find success anyway. I want to show them that they too can achieve anything they set their minds to.*

# CONTENTS

# INTRODUCTION

Let me start with a deceptively simple question: what is a business?

This is something I have been trying to figure out since I was a kid. The answer might seem obvious and simple, but if you can look beyond the traditional definition of a business, a whole new range of possibilities appears.

The traditional definition of a business falls under what I call the "Old Business Model." This style of business requires a storefront, an office building, or perhaps a warehouse with a lease, plus insurance, physical products, inventory, staff, and so much more. In most cases, you need money to get started, you must develop a product, target your audience, and get the word out through marketing and advertising. You may need a certain educational degree or trade skills to advance your business. The process of starting a business can become discouraging to new entrepreneurs because this Old Business Model can be expensive and time consuming.

If the thought of owning your own business gives you anxiety, your only other option is to work for someone else. In this scenario, you are essentially trading your time for money with very little value on your individual skills.

That used to be the only way to do things. Not anymore.

# PART ONE

# THE BUSINESS INSIDE YOU

# CHAPTER ONE

# MY STORY

My journey to entrepreneurship has been anything but straightforward.

## A FARM BOY WITH A DREAM

My mom always says it was a "glorious day" on April 24, 1972, the day I was born. My wife laughs every time she says it, which is almost every time she talks about me.

I was the second child of Jerry and Carolyn Rosser. Both my parents were teachers: my dad was a high school football coach, and my mom taught kindergarten at the local elementary school.

I grew up in Kingsburg, a small town in the San Joaquin Valley of California. The town is so small that if you are driving down Route 99 and sneeze, you might miss it.

I grew up on a twenty-acre farm. My parents were very loving and attentive, and I pretty much had an ideal childhood. However, from the ages of seven to eighteen, I would stick and stumble over my words. I stuttered so badly that, most of the time, I would just not talk. I hated being made fun of, I hated when my dad would tell me to slow down, and I hated being called Stutters at school. My entire childhood, I was embarrassed to speak, and I was terrified of speaking in class.

As a result, I was a very quiet kid who spent a lot of time alone praying, reading, and dreaming. Stuttering hurt my academics, but I tried my best at other things. I joined the football team, I was involved in my local church, and I worked at the local packing house, packing fruit for our local farmers. Kingsburg is big on two things: farming and football.

As the only son, I was often working outside with my dad when he wasn't teaching. When it comes to farming, success is dependent on hard work. I struggled with this. I'm not lazy, but I don't like to work hard either. I watched my parents stress about money all the time, and it used to worry me. I couldn't help thinking there had to be a better way.

When I wasn't working on the farm, I would go on long walks with my dog. The vineyards were a safe place for me because I was alone with my thoughts. In my head, I didn't stutter, and I could just be me. I could think, I could dream, and I could imagine I lived in a different world. While I was daydreaming, I was also praying. I would ask God big questions like "Why can't I stop stuttering? Where does money come from? How can I get more of it?"

It just seemed like if I stopped stuttering, all my problems would be solved. If my parents had more money, all their problems would be solved.

One day, I went for a ride with my dad and his friend George, who was a wealthy farmer in town. I was sitting in the back of the truck, listening to their conversation, and George said to my dad, "Jerry, you want to know the secret of my success?" My ears perked up. This was it. My prayers were about to be answered. Just then, my dad interrupted with some football story and sidetracked the conversation. I sat in the back of the truck, hoping George would bring it up again, but he never did.

### SEARCHING FOR MY PURPOSE

When you come from a small town, most people don't leave. So after high school graduation, I went to the local junior college and lived with my parents. It was during this time that I experienced my first miracle. At nineteen years old, my stutter finally went away.

Most people who stutter into their late teens end up being stutterers for life. I can't explain the joy that I felt when I realized I could speak clearly without stumbling over my words. I still have some hearing issues that prevent me from being completely normal, but I am thankful for the grace God had on me.

As I took college classes, I couldn't decide what I wanted to be when I grew up. So I tried a little of everything: I mowed lawns; I staffed a haunted hayride; I was a youth pastor; I worked at Costco; I even sold vacuums door to door.

My parents always told me I had my grandpa's entrepreneurial spirit because I was always trying to invent things and finding ways to sell anything. On the weekends, I would pick the oranges from my parents' grove, but there was no market for oranges where I lived, so I would drive three hours to San Luis Obispo and sell them at the farmers market there. This was my first experience with taking a product, finding the correct market, and selling it.

One day, I was with my friend at an auto parts store and I found an air freshener made from orange peels that had the perfect orange smell. I took it to the farmers market with me and sprayed it all around the booth. People would walk by and feel compelled to purchase these amazing smelling oranges. It's still one of my greatest marketing tricks of all time.

I tried everything to make money and worked a ton of minimum wage jobs, but they all had very little value. I hated that I was trading so much of my time for so little money. I would constantly think about the amount of time and effort I would put in and the paycheck I would get back. It just never seemed to be worth it. I was always quitting my jobs and looking in the local newspaper for the next one.

Eventually the junior college counselor called me in and said, "Um, Travis, you really need to apply to a university. You honestly can't keep coming here. You've taken almost every class we have." They basically gave me the boot.

I applied to California State University, Fresno. I moved into an apartment near the campus and joined a fraternity. This was my first time away from home, and I pretty much never went to class. With my newfound freedom, I went out with my friends every night, but my recklessness soon earned me a 1.7 GPA. Let's just say I flunked out of Fresno State.

I ended up moving back home. My youth pastor told me about a job as a camp counselor at Hume Lake. At this point, I accepted just about any job that paid, so I took it. This was where I first heard the word *Kajabi* (more on that later). At Hume Lake, I met other counselors who were enrolled at Azusa Pacific University. They had nothing but great things to say about the school, and I wanted to get out of Kingsburg, so I decided to enroll there myself.

At Azusa, I studied marketing and design, and during the summers, I would go back to working as a camp counselor. That was by far my favorite job since all I did was coordinate recreational activities, plus I had free food and board. It was there that I met my first wife.

After I graduated and got married, we moved to Irvine, California. I was in my mid-twenties and I thought I had it made. I had escaped my hometown and achieved my dream of living in Southern California.

Like most college graduates, I got my first job, where I sat in a windowless cubicle all day, Monday through Friday, 8 a.m. to 5 p.m., with a one-hour commute to and from work. I punched in and out, collected my paycheck, and helped my employers become more successful.

I felt stuck. I usually finished my work in less than three hours, then I would spend the rest of the time goofing off. I decided to use that free time productively and taught myself about branding and website design. I started building sites in my spare time. Despite having no formal training, I landed some consulting jobs with bigger companies like Pepsi and Best Buy. Those jobs were fun and challenging, but I still wasn't truly happy.

## STUMBLING ACROSS THE KNOWLEDGE ECONOMY

In 2005, I picked up the newspaper and learned of the tragic death of Corey Rudl. Corey had founded a company called the Internet Marketing Center. I had been subscribed to Corey's email list for a couple of years. I received weekly emails about how much money he was making online. Like every new fast-money idea, I thought it was just a scam.

But the article in the *Orange County Register* spoke of his financial success. I was intrigued. He made all that money online? I needed to find out more. Even though he had passed, his company was still running, and I quickly signed up for their next local event.

The event was in Newport Beach, just twenty minutes from my home. I sat in the back, still cynical about the whole thing, as speakers talked about landing pages, sales pages, email marketing, and the many things you could sell online. One by one, people got up and shared their success stories. There was one guy who made thousands of dollars a month teaching people how to play Madden Football, the video game. I couldn't believe it, thousands of dollars showing people how to play video games!

Then this young kid got up on the stage. He couldn't have been much more than eighteen years old, and he was full of energy and knowledge. As he talked, his story just blew me away.

Jermaine Griggs grew up in the worst part of Long Beach, California, in the same projects that shaped Snoop Dogg and Warren G. His neighborhood was so bad that his mother would tell him to go straight to school and come straight home afterward.

In a random twist of fate, Jermaine's grandmother appeared on *The Price Is Right*, and she won a piano. She taught him how to play when he was a young child. Although he couldn't read sheet music, he learned how to play the piano by ear. He got really, really good at this. He could listen to almost any song, then play it back perfectly.

Jermaine was a hardworking guy and was determined to make something of himself. He tried everything to make money, including selling Avon door to door. One day, he had an idea. He purchased the domain HearandPlay. com and started selling DVDs through the mail, teaching people how to play the piano by ear.

By the time he graduated high school, he had built a successful business. He went to the University of California, Irvine. He bought a home and turned his online business into a multimillion-dollar empire.

During one of the breaks at the conference, I got the courage to go up and introduce myself. Jermaine was already quite successful, and I was just dipping my toe into the idea of making money online. I still wasn't sure if the idea of making money online was another scam or a legitimate way out of the rat race, but for some reason, his story convinced me that this was something real.

Although my partner and I didn't build Kajabi for another five years, the seed was planted. I started looking at the world differently, thinking about how people were making money on the internet and how that process could be improved.

Years later, I met Jermaine again, and we became friends. He is an amazing example of a knowledge entrepreneur. He has so much drive and is constantly consuming information and trying to improve himself. He built something from nothing by just fearlessly trying new things and continually testing his ideas and improving.

There aren't too many Jermaines out there in the world. His drive and ingenuity are something to admire, but there are tons of opportunities to leverage your own talents into the business of your dreams.

## THE BIRTH OF KAJABI

Around 1999, I met my good friend Kenny Rueter. We met at a church group. Everyone else in the group was a teacher. We were the only two who worked in technology, so we naturally gravitated toward each other. We started meeting up for lunch at Chick-fil-A to study the Bible together and talk tech.

All my life, I had grown up with the traditional belief that money was the root of all evil, that loving or wanting money was a bad thing. I didn't believe this and neither did Kenny, so we studied the Bible together, specifically this topic. We would throw out questions like "What did God say about money? Who had it? Who didn't?"

We also worked on projects together. We built software for other people and for ourselves. We tried to build an online tuxedo shop but never made it to launch. We built a scavenger hunt game for Twitter. Then, in 2009, we stumbled upon the idea for Kajabi.

It started with the Crazy Spray. Kenny had this idea for a kids' bike wash. It was made of PVC pipes from Home Depot with sprinkler heads installed. You plug it into your hose, and it's a freestanding structure that kids can ride their bikes through, just like a real car wash.

Kenny built one, and when his neighbors saw it, they wanted one. We thought maybe we could build them and sell them over the internet. But buying the different parts, assembling them, packaging them up, and shipping them out would have been a lot of work. Plus, if the Crazy Spray got traction and became popular, we would eventually need a warehouse. The thought of all the logistics gave me anxiety, and I don't like to say I am lazy, but I knew there had to be a better way.

So instead, we thought, why don't we just teach people how to make them?

We went to Home Depot, and we shot instructional videos. I built a Crazy Spray on my own using only the instructions Kenny wrote—and it worked! So we started a website: CrazySpray.com. We built a shopping cart, uploaded videos, and password-protected the important bits. Even though we were experienced developers, it was difficult to piece the whole system together.

We made some money, and it was cool, but the process was so hard. We thought, "What if there was an easier way to create your own digital products?"

Back then, people were still selling DVDs over the internet instead of hosting videos online. I remembered Jermaine Griggs and how he was still shipping his Hear and Play DVDs through the mail.

What if we could build a platform that made it easy for someone to upload content, put it into categories, build a course, and sell it with an online shopping cart? In this moment, the idea for Kajabi began to come to life.

## LEARNING TO FLY

Why Kajabi?

I bought the domain name for Kajabi many years before we started the company. I was working at Hume Lake, where we played a really fun tug-of-war game called the Kajabi Cancan. I liked the sound of it, so I bought the domain and held on to it. It wasn't until after Kenny and I decided to use it for our new project that I learned the true meaning of the word.

*Kajabi* is an old aboriginal word, meaning "kite hawk." It's also the modern aboriginal word for "airplane." The name fit so well because we loved idea of helping people's business ideas take flight.

Our internal mascot at Kajabi is a duck. A duckling's first flight happens when it tumbles out of the nest. Before it learns to fly, it literally falls. I love that idea of not being perfect, stumbling, falling, but succeeding anyway. That's how my journey has been. The people with the most success on Kajabi are the ones who are raw and honest about themselves and their setbacks.

With this sort of business, there really is no right way to fly. My goal for this book is to inspire you to believe in your own power and knowledge. To have you take flight as you discover the business inside of you. If you're willing to go for it, you might fall and fail a couple of times, but you never know what you may find on the other side.

## SUCCESSES AND STUMBLES

After our lightbulb moment with the Crazy Spray, we got serious about building a platform that would make it easy to sell knowledge. We reached out to an online marketer named Andy Jenkins. Kenny and I drove down to San Diego and pitched him our idea for Kajabi. Andy was in the process of developing a new product. He was excited about the idea, and together, we partnered to bring the first version of Kajabi to life.

Andy built his course, called the Video Boss, which was about marketing and how to do online videos. We built the first version of Kajabi to handle all his content. In February 2010, Andy launched his product using Kajabi and sold his course to thousands of people. He made so much money it kind of blew our minds. The thing we built had worked!

With Andy's help, we reached out to other people like Frank Kern, Jeff Walker, and eventually Brendon Burchard, who are all well-known in the internet marketing space. With bigger names attached to our product, people in the online marketing space really started sitting up and taking notice. In October 2010, we officially launched Kajabi and thousands of people started signing up right off the bat. That first year, we saw our customers make millions of dollars on our platform, which absolutely blew our minds.

It wasn't all smooth sailing, though. Kenny and I were both working full-time jobs in addition to running Kajabi. We would work all day, then sometimes all night.

We launched the site on a Thursday. Thousands of people signed up, and they obviously had a lot of questions. We had hired a great team in the Philippines to take care of our customer service, but we forgot that the Philippines is almost a full day ahead of the United States. This became a huge problem because on Thursday evening, their Friday night, they all left for the weekend. Meanwhile, thousands of help tickets started flooding in.

All day Friday, we didn't notice that our Filipino help desk wasn't responding to the help tickets. I was at my kid's soccer game on Saturday morning when Kenny frantically called to tell me we had a major problem. I went over to his house, set up every computer we could find on the kitchen table, and started answering thousands of help tickets. There were so many tickets that needed attention that we asked family, friends, and even neighbors to help us.

It was stressful, but we got through it. By the next week, the stress had eased a bit, but I still had so much pent-up anxiety. So much so, that one morning I sat down in my office and felt my whole chest tighten. I was convinced I was having a heart attack and was going to die. I rushed to the emergency room, where I was diagnosed with an anxiety attack.

I pushed myself so far out of my comfort zone that creating Kajabi almost killed me, but it was worth it.

Starting a business was hard, but it has also been very rewarding. Kajabi courses have changed people's lives. I know this for a fact because one dramatically changed mine. I will share that story later.

## KAJABI TODAY

This year Kajabi celebrates its eighth anniversary. A business that started with two strangers meeting at church now employs over thirty people.

In 2015, we completely rebuilt the entire Kajabi system from scratch. After learning more about how people used the software, we added new features to make it one of the easiest ways to create, market, and sell online courses. With the success of earlier users, more and more people have signed up to sell their courses.

At the time of this writing, Kajabi customers have collectively made more than half a billion dollars selling their knowledge online. Many knowledge entrepreneurs have made over a million dollars, and some of our biggest customers have made tens of millions of dollars. I will be telling some of their stories later in the book.

# CHAPTER TWO

# THE STORY OF KNOWLEDGE CAPITAL

*The Global E-Learning Market...accounted for $165.21 billion in 2017, and is expected to reach $275.1 billion by 2022...*

*The key factors that are favoring the market growth are flexibility in learning, low cost, and easy accessibility...*

*Moreover, escalation in the number of internet users and growing access of broadband pooled with mobile phones with online capabilities are also fueling market growth.*

—ORBIS RESEARCH, JUNE 15, 2017[1]

---

1  Reuters, "Global E-Learning Market 2017 to Boom $275.10 Billion Value by 2022 at a CAGR of 7.5%: Orbis Research." Last modified June 15, 2017. https://www.reuters.com/brandfeatures/venture-capital/article?id=11353

## THE OLD-SCHOOL WAY

Traditionally, to become successful, you went to college, studied to become an expert in one subject, got a job in that field, and hopefully got paid a high salary. To this day, many people still believe this is the only way to become successful. The lie society tells us from early childhood is that you need a degree to get a job in order to have a decent life. In other words, your level of education determines your quality of life.

Yes, there are some important occupations where degrees are essential, like doctors, lawyers, and engineers. Unfortunately, these degrees also come with big student loans, and you can spend years paying them off.

Oftentimes, people aimlessly go through the motions of college without a plan for what to do after graduation. Most students enter college undeclared and just start taking classes trying to find their passion while accumulating debt. I was one of them.

According to an article in *Forbes*:

Student loan debt is now the second highest consumer debt category...there are more than 44 million borrowers with $1.3 trillion in student loan debt in the US alone.

The average student in the class of 2016 has $37,172 in student loan debt.[2]

From our very first day of preschool, we are conditioned to always be looking toward the next level of schooling. When we're in elementary school, we're looking forward to middle school. When we're in middle school, we're looking forward to high school. In high school, we're looking forward to college. In college, we're looking forward to graduation, possibly graduate school ending with the goal of finding a job. Then when you finally find that elusive job, what do you have to look forward to?

Here is a radical thought: maybe completing school and finding a good job isn't the ultimate purpose in life. Yes, we all need money to live, and a job helps to pay the bills. But I am here to tell you that there are other ways to make money. There are other paths you can follow. For me, the question was always: how can I expand beyond just my job and use the knowledge that I have? I want to make more money and have a more fulfilling life rather than feeling trapped in a cubicle all day.

The process of employment used to be purely external; it was something that happened to you and around you.

2    Zack Friedman, "Student Loan Debt In 2017: A $1.3 Trillion Crisis," Forbes.com. Last modified February 21, 2017. https://www.forbes.com/sites/zackfriedman/2017/02/21/student-loan-debt-statistics-2017/#a49b1bc5daba

You would put in your time and receive a paycheck. The more time you put in, the more you might have advanced within a predetermined structure. Everyone has heard the expressions "moving up the corporate ladder" or "working toward that corner office." But moving up the ladder could take years. Honestly, this is a great time to be alive because the internet has completely changed all of this.

## WELCOME TO THE KNOWLEDGE ECONOMY

When we started Kajabi, I had a theory. I thought that everyone must be good at something. If there were just an easy way to share and monetize those skills, then anyone could own their own business.

Eight years on, this theory has been proven. The customers who use our online platform to sell their knowledge online have made over half a billion dollars collectively. I like to call them Knowledge Entrepreneurs.

They made their money using a new business model centered on the idea that every single person has a business inside of them by virtue of their own unique past experiences and personal knowledge.

This new business model releases individuals from the restrictions of the old-fashioned brick-and-mortar business model. Anyone can start a business and become their own boss. And they can do it from the comfort of their own home, just by harnessing the skills they already have.

In the new Knowledge Economy, what you know is now your most valuable resource. Everything you've learned, everything you've been through, everything you're good at, and everything you are passionate about are your potential assets. It's great to have a retirement fund or own real estate, but knowledge itself can be a much more valuable asset. The reason why it's so valuable is because it belongs solely to you and can never be stolen or reproduced. If you learn how to cultivate that valuable knowledge into a product or service, it can generate income, which can then transform you into a knowledge entrepreneur.

I like to sometimes joke that this process is "turning what you know into dough." Throughout your life, you've collected experiences: struggles, pains, passions, or talents that you have developed and excelled at. Now you can take that knowledge and those experiences, and turn them into an income-generating business.

For example, let's say you bake the best chocolate chip cookies in the entire world. Using the Old Business Model, you might decide to start a bakery and be forced to undergo all the trials and tribulations of launching a brick-and-mortar business. What if, instead, you used the internet to teach people how to bake the perfect cookie themselves? It involves less hassle, fewer startup costs, and less work. Instead of just reaching a few thousand customers in your area, you could potentially market your product to millions of people around the world.

Yes, people have been sharing their secrets and how-to videos on YouTube for years, but most of them have simply been giving away their knowledge for free. I will teach you how to get paid for your knowledge.

The Knowledge Economy changes our conceptions of where money comes from and how to get more of it. Entrepreneurs are freed from the old model of exchanging time for money. Instead of just selling your product or service to the people around you, thanks to the internet, you are now anywhere and everywhere. Someone can consume your knowledge in the middle of the night, halfway around the world. The internet offers a broad spectrum of new tools for starting and growing an online business.

## THE EVOLUTION OF KNOWLEDGE ONLINE

Originally, the only way to transfer knowledge was via word of mouth. If you wanted to learn a skill, a trade, or a craft, you would find the local expert and ask them to teach you. You could only reach the experts in your immediate village or surrounding areas. Some skills were passed down by family members, but learning the skill set took place via an apprenticeship.

Then over time, there was the written word: books, newspapers, telegraphs. Still, if you needed to know something specific, someone had to connect you with that piece of information.

Today, the internet is the first place we turn to for information, whether it be research, asking a question, watching a video, reading an article, or discovering new ideas. This wasn't always the case.

When the internet first came into general use, it was a huge repository of random information. In the beginning, everything was just dumped into a disorganized space. There was lots of static information. It was cold, impersonal, and lacking in human connection. The amount of information without organization was overwhelming.

Yahoo started organizing web pages by categories. Then Google started to rank search results by relevance. Now that the internet wasn't just a repository of information, it started to become a source of actual knowledge.

Information and knowledge are two separate concepts. Information is cold and impersonal. It's facts and data without human connection. Knowledge is the smart, warm, personal side of information. Behind it is a real person, someone who knows how to do something and is willing to show you how. Picture the village expert who learned a skill or trade through trial and error and now wants to pass down their knowledge to you.

Today, the internet is the main marketplace for knowledge capital. The internet is literally everywhere: it's on our phones and in our pockets. We all participate in it every single day. If you search for an answer on Google, you are benefitting from knowledge capital. You are the recipient of someone else's knowledge that they took the time to share online.

The internet has broken all the barriers to knowledge acquisition. Now you can connect with someone in a part of the world you've never even visited and convey meaningful knowledge to them. You can make online courses, downloadable documents, ebooks, and all kinds of digital content.

Knowledge is easily transferred online. If you don't know how to do something, you pull up a YouTube video and someone demonstrates it for you. So many people want to share what they have learned. It's pretty simple: someone knew how to do something, they made a cool video, you watched it, and now you know how to do it too. You experienced a transaction where knowledge was transferred between two people who have never even met. Amazing. Now the world is your village and the experts are everywhere.

## THIS IS JUST THE BEGINNING

We are still in the infancy of the Knowledge Economy. As broadband spreads, as more people have smartphones, and as technology becomes cheaper and more accessible, more people are going to share, and more people are going to be looking for answers on the internet.

There will be more people just like you who say, "Wow, I should really do this. Now is the time." This is the beginning of a new era of exchanging knowledge. It's just barely started, and there's so much more to come.

The future of the internet is fostering new connections. We are connecting daily about topics we care about or are struggling with. We look for answers online when we're sick or suffering, and we connect with others who have been through the same struggles. When you find real, authentic people on the other side, suddenly, you relax and think, "Wow, here's someone else who knows about this topic and has been through it." We no longer feel alone in this big world.

To be successful on the internet, however, you do need to

be authentic. Some people tout the idea of "fake it until you make it," but I personally hate that. I prefer to say, "Be it until you achieve it." Be yourself, be vulnerable, and be genuine because people will always spot a fake. The longer people use the internet, the more they crave authenticity. People will buy from you when you are your true self, so don't be fake, just be you.

When someone knows you, likes you, and trusts you, they'll buy from you. In fact, if you keep helping them and giving them value, they will become a customer for life.

As you are reading, where does your life story fit in all of this? Can you imagine how the things you've been through, the troubles you've overcome, or the things you've become good at, can somehow impact someone else's life? There is really no telling how far this new movement could take you. This is the future of knowledge capital.

## BECOME A KNOWLEDGE ENTREPRENEUR

Knowledge entrepreneurship is the idea that every single person has experiences that make them an expert in their own unique niche. By leaning deep into this expertise, you can open doors you never knew existed. You can build a lucrative business, as well as benefit the wider community, and enrich other people's lives just by adding your knowledge to the world.

As a knowledge entrepreneur, you will capitalize on your specific niche, the more distinctive the better. Think left-handed golfing, gluten-free baking, or tapping meditation. We have a customer at Kajabi, who I will talk about more later, who built an entire business not just on nutrition, but intermittent fasting.

The special thing about this idea is that your life's journey, your individuality, your personality, your character all infuse your business with a unique flavor that allows you to connect with certain people. Maybe not with everyone, maybe just a small group, but it won't matter because your voice will resonate so strongly in that small group that it can truly be a catalyst to creating a million-dollar business.

Not only will you be helping people and making money, you will be building a more fulfilling professional and personal life for yourself. When you take what you know and turn it into a business, the passion and energy that comes from helping other people will enrich your own life in a new way.

## YOU, INC.

My goal in writing this book is to open people's minds to the idea of the business inside you, what I like to call You, Incorporated.

I believe that every single person has something special

inside of them. Either they're born with it, or they acquire it. This special talent or gift can grow throughout their life, through good and bad experiences. It can eventually become an asset they can share with the rest of the world. That's the business inside you.

I love meeting new people and finding out what they have to share. What's the business lurking inside of them? This is a big part of why I co-founded Kajabi.

I believe in the business inside of you because I have personally witnessed this phenomenon. The people who are on Kajabi have used their knowledge capital to exponentially improve the quality of their lives.

And you can do it too!

# CHAPTER THREE

# YOU ARE THE HERO OF YOUR STORY

As the great Jay-Z once said, "I'm not a businessman. I'm a business, man."

This quote has stuck with me for years. I love the concept that you are not just someone who runs a business, but what's inside of you *is* the business.

When you realize this fundamental truth, then you are ready to begin this amazing journey. It won't always be a straight line to success, but you will find yourself going places and doing things you never thought you could do.

This is about being the driving force to make changes in your own life. In Chapter One, I talked about my struggles and the things I wanted to change in my life. Sometimes I directly caused the changes, and sometimes things eventually changed because of my attitude.

The people who will come away from this book ready for success are those willing to act on it. Think about Jermaine Griggs. He had everything against him, but he kept going because he knew that nobody else was responsible for the course of his life. He didn't blame anybody for his situation. He had goals in mind and just took action.

You are the only one that is going to help you get out of your current situation. Only you can go down the path of your dreams. I know a lot of people that get stuck and think they can't move forward. They make nonstop excuses as to why they have to stay in their current situation. But, if you are serious about changing your life, you need to get rid of the excuses. Open your mind to the possibilities of becoming a Knowledge Entrepreneur. You will be amazed where this could take you.

Your mistakes that you make along the way are the foundation of your story and business. My stuttering, my struggling in school, and my going through a divorce are all part of who I am. How I approach everything in my life is because of those struggles and weaknesses.

This is revolutionary. It means that your own weaknesses

can become your greatest strengths. Everything you experience and learn throughout life is your education. For example, if you are disorganized or suffer from ADD, then the special tools and adaptations you've created to help you focus are a huge resource. You could become an expert on dealing with that weakness, and I am sure someone out there wants to know how you did it.

## DISCOVERING YOUR BUSINESS

Now I would like to start guiding you through the process of understanding and thinking about your story. Let's figure out how it might relate to a potential business idea.

Here are some questions to ask yourself as you examine your life. The answers to these questions are potentially the foundation of what kind of business is inside of you. They help you take inventory of your experiences, your gifts, and the unique message you could potentially share.

### WHAT HAS YOUR LIFE LOOKED LIKE UP TO THIS POINT?

Think about your childhood, your past, all the important events in your life up until now. Were your parents married or divorced? Are you married, single, divorced, or widowed? What kind of job do you currently have? Did you survive something? Did you experience a tragedy?

Did you overcome something? Have you won any special awards for your talents?

## WHAT DO YOU WANT YOUR LIFE TO LOOK LIKE?

When I was a kid, all I wanted was to stop stuttering. My parents tried just about everything. I was enrolled in speech therapy, went to counseling, did all the things you are supposed to do, and it just wasn't working for me. For years, I continued to stick and stumble over my words despite all the programs they put me in. Regardless of what my teachers told my parents, I never stopped dreaming of a future where I didn't stutter. As an adult, I know it sounded like a ridiculous dream, but as a kid, nothing was impossible. And one day, a miracle happened, and I stopped stuttering.

This is what you need to do. Take out a piece of paper right now and write down the things you dream about: *I want a house. I want to be my own boss. I want to drive a Porsche. I want to be debt free. I want a million dollars.* Don't worry about what's possible. Just dream of your future. Dream with the limitless mind of a child, and let the miracle happen in your life.

## WHERE DO YOU WANT TO GO?

Where do you want to go in life? Do you want to own your

own business? Do you want to travel the world with your family? Do you want to get out of the cubicle for good? Do you want to change people's lives?

Imagine the possibilities and start envisioning your future.

This is the beginning of everything. You are picking your destination and inputting that destination into your internal GPS. You know that system in your car that helps you get places? Well, what happens when you type something into your GPS? It gives you directions, right? And what happens if you make a wrong turn? If you're like me, you probably beat yourself up internally. But your GPS simply tells you, "Make a U-turn, and proceed to the route."

That is how dreams are too. If you are set on a dream and you head toward it, even if you miss it, life is still going to tell you to turn around and proceed to the route.

## WHERE ARE YOU NOW?

Assess your current situation and make a list of the things you are passionate about, the things that you find joy in and the things you can't stop talking about. Here are some examples: I like to mountain bike. I like making crafts with my kids. I'm good at designing websites. I'm good at talking to people. I'm good at yoga. I'm the best salesperson in my company. I make amazing gluten-free cookies.

It's important to take stock of your weaknesses along with your strengths. Don't feel ashamed about your failures because your failures can become your biggest life lessons. For example, my wife, Paola, incurred massive credit card debt while in college. For years, she struggled, living paycheck to paycheck, and never being able to pay down her debts. She began to research different ways to pay off her credit cards, even though she failed multiple times, eventually she put together a system that worked for her, and now she teaches others how to do the same.

What are some things you've failed at?

## WHAT WILL YOU NEED TO CHANGE TO GET THERE?

This is important. This is when you start to build your roadmap. You know where you want to go, so now we need to figure out how to get there.

You might ask yourself some of these questions: Do I need to get up earlier? Do I need to start writing down my ideas? Do I need to learn something new? Do I need to go to an event?

When you start asking the right questions, you will somehow get the right answers. It's like the GPS telling you to make a U-turn. I like to think of our internal GPS as

God Pushing Softly. Whether it's God or the universe or instinct, listen to it because it will guide you in the right direction. What if you listened to your inner voice? What might happen?

## IS YOUR STORY VALUABLE?

Right away, I'm going to answer this one for you. Yes, your story is valuable.

Everyone has a story to tell, and it's important to find the most valuable elements of your story. If you can't, find someone close to you who can help you—your mom or dad, your spouse, your brother or sister, or anyone you can trust. Go have dinner with that person. Sit down and talk about your story. Ask them, "Hey, what's unique about my story?"

## CAN YOUR STORY CHANGE SOMEONE'S LIFE?

Keith Kalfas teaches a course about how to start your own landscaping business. He's the number-one leader on social media for the term *landscaping*.

On the surface, his topic seems very innocuous. He teaches topics like picking a lawn mower or dealing with trimming trees. But in between nuggets of information, Keith is his own hilarious self. He talks about his life, his struggles, and mistakes. Keith is great at connecting with people.

Multiple people have contacted him and said, "Keith, I was at the end of my rope. I was on the internet late at night. I don't even know how I found your videos. But I watched them, and you made me laugh. I was going to give up. I was literally going to take my life, but because of your message and story, I didn't."

It's crazy to think that in all of this—in talking about business and all the things you want—your story could literally save someone's life. That's powerful. That's why you should share, no matter what struggle comes in front of you, whether it's stuttering like me or self-doubt or something else. Your story can change lives and possibly save some.

## CONNECTING THE DOTS

This book is meant to help you connect all these pieces and find your story so you can discover this business inside of you.

In Chapter Four you will find a set of tools for uncovering your own unique expertise. These will help you to identify some potential ideas for your business. It's almost like mining your own brain for treasure, and I'm going to help you dig.

Then, in Chapters 5 through 8, I will introduce a wide

range of successful knowledge entrepreneurs. These stories will hopefully serve as an inspiration for developing your own personal brand and knowledge capital. Some of these stories are going to blow your mind because either the people are teaching something very unique and have had success, or they have gone from nothing to becoming millionaires. It's really, really powerful.

Then, in Chapters 9 and 10, we will talk about how to put your idea into motion and create a business that is actually profitable.

Let's get started.

# PART TWO

# FROM KNOWLEDGE TO A BUSINESS

# CHAPTER FOUR

# DISCOVER YOUR KNOWLEDGE NICHE

Today, Nicole Begley is a pet photographer, but she didn't start out that way. For thirteen years, she was a trainer at the zoo, taking care of monkeys, birds, and other animals. After she had her second child, she found that the stresses of middle management and demands of working full time hours were too much. She no longer loved her job and wanted to spend more time with her young children.

So she decided to turn her photography hobby into a business. She began with families and pets, and soon realized she liked photographing pets a lot more. She realized that her background in working with animals made her an expert in dealing with and photographing pets.

Then she started teaching other people how to take pictures of their pets. She recognized an opportunity not just to teach photography skills but to teach others how to start their own pet photography business. Now, not only is she an expert pet photographer, but she also makes a living helping others start their own similar companies.

Nicole found the perfect union. She is a great animal photographer and uses her unique knowledge to help other people. She found her knowledge niche. Nicole no longer works at the zoo. She travels all over the world, conducts pet photography workshops, and makes a living sharing her knowledge. You can see her work and courses at www.nicolebegleyphotography.com.

## DISCOVERING YOUR KNOWLEDGE NICHE

The first step to building your own knowledge capital business is finding your own knowledge niche.

A niche in this context is a subset of information, a very specific category or interest. The more specific your niche, the better. For example, golfing is a very broad niche, but left-handed golfing is a unique, more specific topic. When you narrow your niche down to a very precise level, it becomes easier to find a group of people who share the same interest. In that way, a niche represents the group of people you are trying to connect with, also known as your audience.

Once you find your niche, you can create a powerful and successful business. That niche is the diamond right under your nose.

Have you heard the great parable by Russell H. Conwell called "Acres of Diamonds"? When I hear stories about how customers discover their niches, this story always comes to mind.

In "Acres of Diamonds," Conwell tells the story of a farmer in Africa who is wealthy and content until he hears that his country has diamonds. He sells his farm and goes out to search for diamonds. He spends his entire life searching and finds nothing. Despondent, he drowns, and later, it's discovered that his original property, the one he sold at the beginning of the story, was sprinkled with diamonds. The moral of the story is that, oftentimes, we don't recognize our greatest assets even when they are right under our nose.

I think a lot of people lack the perspective to recognize their personal gifts, talents, or skills. The trick is to identify the diamond within you before it's too late.

Steve Jobs once said, "Your life is a series of dots. You

just have to trust they will all get connected." I hope this book helps you look at some of the dots in your life and start connecting them.

## THE FOUR PS OF EXPERTISE

To help you find your own special niche, I'd like to introduce the Four Ps of Expertise: profession, passion, pain, and problem. Most people have an expertise that falls into one of these categories, but they are not mutually exclusive, and they often overlap. By understanding each category, you can start to consider what aspects of your life could best serve as a source for finding your knowledge niche.

### PROFESSION

Profession means more than just your job. It includes any skills or special traits you have that are related to your job. If you're an accountant, you might expect to simply teach accounting, but there is likely a far more specific niche within the world of accounting. What software do you use for your job? Are you notably talented at working with Excel?

Maybe you work in real estate and you're really good at property management. Or maybe you work in the marketing department and you're infamous for your design techniques. Or maybe you are a teacher and you have the best way to learn statistics. Maybe you hate your job, but you love planning the office Christmas party each year. There is a reason your heart leaps when that time of year comes around: it's trying to tell you there is a business there. That's what we're looking for. The passion that makes us want to work all night long, then get up in the morning and work some more. You can't fake that.

Another way to approach the question of profession is: What are you innately good at? What comes naturally to you? It could be math, public speaking, cooking, or stretching. That one thing could be anything. What would someone pay you to do for them? Do their taxes, teach them nutrition, improve their range of motion? Most people take what they already know for granted. The key is to figure out what you're naturally good at and then find an audience for it.

Even if you are bored and hate your job, it can serve as a source for a profitable knowledge business. The trick is to change it, tweak it, and make it work for you instead of you working for it.

Jon Acampora worked as an analyst. He found his actual job boring, but there was one thing he really enjoyed. He loved working with the computer program Excel. He became an expert at the programming and automatic scripts and eventually knew how to make the program do just about anything.

Soon enough, Jon found himself training other people. Every time someone was stuck, they would come by and ask for a tutorial. Jon started blogging about Excel outside of work. He started making downloadable Excel templates and programs that he gave away in exchange for an email address. After a while, he had a pretty significant email list and decided to launch his own course. He built his website ExcelCampus.com.

Sure enough, it sold over and over again. At this point, Jon has made over six figures teaching Excel. He quit his boring job, became his own boss, and now he is a knowledge entrepreneur. He took an element from his previously boring profession and turned it into a job he loves. Now Jon gets to help people all around the world.

Ask yourself, is there something at your job that you are known for being the expert at? Something people are constantly asking you to do or help with? There's a reason for this: the seeds have already been planted in your life. It's time to start recognizing them.


PASSION

The second P is for passion. This is all about what you love to do for fun. The stuff that energizes you so much that you do it for free. You might even spend money doing it. These things might be a little easier to identify than the previous category because they are your hobbies. It's very possible that you could be making money from the very thing you love to do in your free time.

Think about how you spend your Saturdays: What's your favorite thing to do on your day off? Do you play golf? Mountain bike? Ride horses? Build old car engines? Fly drones? Take pictures? Every single one of those passions could potentially turn into a knowledge business.

It's a myth that hobbies are strictly for fun. They can absolutely be monetized.

Here's a helpful way to shift your perspective: What parts of your hobby cost you money? For example, I love flying drones. My wife thinks it's crazy because I'm a grown man, but I love it. I am constantly watching videos on YouTube about drones. The experts out there are showing me which ones to buy, how to fly them, how to take pictures with them, and more. If one of these people could show others how to use their drones in a business capacity, say roof inspections or real estate videos, then they would be onto a great business idea.

## PAIN

The next P is pain. Pain refers to both physical pain and severe emotional pain. Think devastating life events.

How can pain be a source of expertise or knowledge? Oftentimes, when someone struggles with pain in their life, they learn tools and strategies to help them manage and overcome their issues. Some people have endured unimaginable pain and survived it. When you go through tragic life events and later you see someone else suffering, you want to help.

Pain, along with the fourth P, problems, can be one of the most powerful sources of expertise. All of us have gone through pain in our lives. What if you could turn that experience into something positive? Maybe it can bring some purpose to the fact you went through it at all.

My pastor, Rick Warren, wrote the book *The Purpose Driven Life*. He always says you can become bitter or you can become better. I know we all want to become better because becoming bitter is terrible. Sometimes the bitterness can be worse than the original pain. Maybe you can turn your pain into purpose. After you have grieved and healed, you can turn an experience that felt devastating into something positive.

Many Kajabi courses have changed people's lives. I know this for a fact because one dramatically changed mine.

I was unhappily married for years but didn't feel like divorce was an option, given my religious background. I was always depressed and lacking in energy. My business was finally successful, but I still felt like there was something wrong with me. I was in a dark place and desperate for answers.

One day, I stumbled across a guy on YouTube. He was foulmouthed, yelled a lot, but he encouraged men to rebuild their lives. He asked men to be honest, focus on their families, and grow their businesses. I had felt so alone, and yet here was this man giving me hope. His name was Garrett J. White. I searched for more of his videos and discovered that he offered a course on Kajabi. Garrett's Kajabi course was called Wake Up Warrior. What are the odds?

Sometime in 2012, I met Garrett at an event. We chatted a bit, and I told him how his videos had helped me. As we talked about what was going on in my life, he predicted that one day I would get a divorce and start over. I honestly didn't believe him since there was no way I would even consider divorce at that point.

But a year later, just as he predicted, my marriage fell apart. We filed for divorce, and I was devastated. I had been married for fifteen years and had two wonderful sons. My life changed drastically overnight. I moved out of our home with only a small bag of clothes into a small condo. For months, I was alone and completely depressed.

After finally reaching my breaking point, I signed up for Warrior Week, Garrett's in-person event in Laguna Beach.

The event was set up like boot camp. There was an intense focus on your physical body, your business, your love life, and your spiritual life. It was a bunch of men encouraging each other to be better versions of themselves. That weekend, I met five guys who have become lifelong friends. The whole experience absolutely changed my life. Wake Up Warrior helped me find my purpose and gave me confidence to rebuild my life. I recently found the love of my life and got remarried. And not only were those five guys my groomsmen, but Garrett J. White also attended our wedding. You can learn more about Wake Up Warrior on warriorweek.com.

Today, when I look at my beautiful wife, I am so happy to have been given a second chance at happiness. I still can't believe that someone used the platform I had created to make a course that would ultimately change my own life. What are the odds of this happening? I felt like it was all predestined.

If you find your knowledge business in the Pain category, you can totally change people's lives. You can help people by providing them comfort, relief, or hope. The mental challenge here is looking at this knowledge as a business because people are reluctant to charge money to help other people. The thing is, when you start providing this kind of value on a larger scale, it takes up more and more of your time, to where it becomes a job. If you could get paid to do this, you could put all your energy into helping others instead of working at a less meaningful job. Think about how many more people you could reach if you did this full time? You could actually reach people across the world with your message of survival. But to do that, you must be willing to charge for your knowledge. Trust me, people who are suffering are willing to pay for your knowledge and expertise.

## PROBLEMS

The final P is for problems. This one overlaps a bit with pain, but they are different. Think of a problem as something that was a struggle or a mistake. It didn't necessarily involve physical pain, and it wasn't necessarily emotionally devastating, but it wasn't pleasant either. The major difference here is that you overcome pain, but you fix a problem. Examples would include being in debt, losing a job, or dating issues. The fix to the problem is whatever adjustments you made that led you to a positive outcome.

Again, perhaps you have been chosen to go through this

struggle so that you can guide others through their journeys by offering solutions, comfort, and encouragement. Often, we look at our weaknesses and mistakes as shortcomings. What if we looked at them as gifts?

Look at your problems as opportunities for you to learn something new, to figure something out, to find a solution and fix the problem. The myth that we need to be social-media perfect is ridiculous. Every day on Facebook or Instagram, we see someone posting the perfect smile with the perfect angle in the perfect place. Sometimes I feel like people go to a place, pose, get the perfect picture, leave, and don't even do the thing they say they're doing. It sucks that our world has come to this. Remember that the key to knowledge capital and building your online business is authenticity. You must be transparent. You must be real. Authenticity is huge, especially when your knowledge is going to come from a problem you faced. It will literally be the foundation for your knowledge business to work.

If you're not authentic and aren't able to show your mistakes and problems, others are not going to trust you. They're going to think, "This person is fake. Why would I want a fake person trying to help me?" When you are someone who has been there, done that, and has empathy and understanding, others will want to connect with you. Being real is what is required to connect with potential customers. Being open about your problems is the way to help others.

As I said in the pain section, you can make money here too. Again, you may have to change your perspective and be okay with making money from this. Once it becomes your full-time business, your full focus, you will be able to help more people. You will be able to make a bigger difference and have more of an impact on the world.

**THE PURPOSE DIAGRAM**

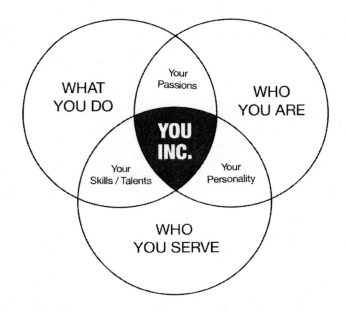

The Purpose Diagram was created by Scott Perry, a Kajabi customer who brands himself as the Stoic Guitarist. I have altered the diagram a little for the book, but the concept is brilliant. It's a tool for identifying your purpose.

Everybody is trying to figure out their purpose in life, and it's not always easy to identify, but this diagram helps. Finding your purpose is important because it can help guide you through this journey.

The first circle on the left is *what we do*: it includes our job, our profession, our career. It's what we get paid for. It's the thing you do that helps you pay the bills. It may be what you went to school for.

The far-right circle is *who we are*: it includes our hobbies, our interests, our passions, and the things we do for fun. This circle also encompasses the challenges, pain, and problems you have overcome in your life.

The circle at the bottom is *those you serve*: communities of people you impact by what you do and who you are. It includes your coworkers, your bosses, and your clients, or anyone else you might help. Where these circles intersect is where you find your talent, your vocation, and your character.

Let's talk about where these circles intersect. The overlap between *what you do* and *who you serve* is easy to pin down. It's your job and your clients and coworkers. Similarly, what you do and who you are also overlap. This is where you find your talents. Things you are naturally good at, like analytic thinking or writing or public speaking. It's very important to understand what your talents are.

Another interesting overlap is where *who you are* crosses with *who you serve*. This is where you find your character. This is what you bring to the table when you are doing your job: humor, organization, a type A personality, etc. As you were reading earlier, you may have thought, "Who is going to consider me as an expert? Who is going to listen to me?" These are your unique traits that will make potential customers want to give you a chance.

Here's the beauty of this diagram: where all three circles come together is where your power is. It is where you find your purpose.

This is the most powerful source to mine. This is where the sellable knowledge has been hidden. This is where the diamond is. You may not have noticed it was there before because you've been so distracted by only focusing on one circle. Each circle on its own is not powerful enough. How they all come together is the where the true power is.

Think about this: Do you regularly get questions from coworkers at work? Do you regularly feel good inside when you do a certain hobby? When this happens, your soul is trying to tell you, "Hey, this is it. This is your aha moment. This is your purpose."

## THE NEXT STEPS

So how do you discover your knowledge niche?

First, let's take a deep dive into some stories of knowledge entrepreneurs from each of these four categories. Chapters 5 through 8 will give you tons of examples of people who turned their profession, passion, pain, or problem into businesses. You will quickly see how each category is rich with possibilities for sellable products. At the end of each chapter, I will walk you through exercises for uncovering your own knowledge niche.

# CHAPTER FIVE

# PROFESSION AS KNOWLEDGE

This chapter presents stories of knowledge entrepreneurs whose knowledge products were derived directly from their professional expertise.

As you read through these stories, try to keep in mind that people want to know what you know. Think about the tools you use, the unique skills you've developed, and how you can use information you already possess to educate others.

## LEAH MCHENRY: FROM STAY-AT-HOME MOM TO MUSIC MARKETING GURU

Leah McHenry is a stay-at-home mom from Canada with five children. Her husband worked construction while she stayed home, and money was tight. They did everything they could to make ends meet, and at one point, they became very close to financial ruin.

Leah started an online music career in a very specific niche. She plays Celtic metal music. She didn't have a label, but she had released a few albums online herself. She also sold niche merchandise related to her genre, like T-shirts, artwork, swords, and other items. She found a whole bunch of other ways to monetize her niche and did quite well. She was making good money without having to go on the road or deal with a record label, and she was doing it all from home.

People started asking her how she marketed her business so well. At first, she thought she would write an ebook. She spent a lot of time writing down all her tips and putting them into a PDF. Then she found Chalene Johnson.

Chalene Johnson is a fitness entrepreneur who talks a lot about marketing, and she inspired Leah to put aside the ebook. Instead, Leah pursued the idea of a music marketing course, which led her to Kajabi.

The first week after Leah's course launched, she made $30,000. Within months, her business had grown exponentially. By the time I met Leah, she had been using Kajabi for a year, and her course was so successful that her husband had quit his job. Today he stays home and helps her with her business. They're no longer in financial straits, and she told me that her marriage has improved because now they can spend more time together.

This is another reason why it is so important for you to find your purpose and do something about it. You cannot wait for someone else to change your life or for someone else to give you a chance and make your dreams happen. It must be you. You need to make the moves to make your dreams come true.

You can find Leah's course at SaavyMusicianAcademy. com.

## DR. V: CHANGING LIVES WITH POSTSURGERY ADVICE

Dr. Duc Vuong, or Dr. V, as he often goes by, is a bariatric surgeon and weight-loss expert. More than that, he's a man with a mission to change the entire medical industry's approach to health and well-being.

Dr. V specializes in stomach stapling, lap-band surgery, and gastric-sleeve surgery, all procedures that help people lose weight. However, he has witnessed that the surgery itself is often just a Band-Aid for deeper problems. If his patients don't change their attitude and perspective toward food and wellness, they have a high probability of returning to the same weight or more. This kind of relapse can be devastating.

He has noticed drastically different postsurgery outcomes with patients that focus on overhauling their entire lifestyle. He wanted to help people make these changes, so he started offering courses to help coach people postsurgery. His course has been very successful, and his patients' success rates have gone up. He now calls himself "The Support Surgeon." He envisions a movement in which all doctors offer this kind of postsurgery/posttreatment support. He is still testing his findings and is working on the medical research to pin down the results. He's also created an online subscription plan that enables him to keep the education and interaction ongoing since it's a lifelong struggle.

Dr. V recognized a problem in his profession and saw a way to respond. That's powerful, because he could have just kept doing surgeries and made a very good living that way. Instead, he thought, "No, I have to do something. I have to help people beyond the surgery."

You can see Dr. V's work www.DucVuong.com.

## KEITH KALFAS: FROM LANDSCAPING TO YOUTUBE

We talked a bit about Keith Kalfas in Chapter Three and how his landscaping business has literally changed people's lives.

Growing up, Keith had several businesses. He ran a landscaping business but also had other jobs. He had been taught to just keep working harder and harder. Eventually, he thought, "This is nuts."

In his videos today, Keith tells stories of starting his landscaping business. He says, "I bought this beat-up old truck and used lawn mower, and I just went. I didn't know how to get a customer or what I was doing." He just went and did it.

Keith lives just outside of Detroit, Michigan. When the cold months arrived, his landscaping business would come to a halt, so he had to find other ways to make money. Keith was a fan of Brendon Burchard, an incredible motivational speaker and marketing expert. His books and training programs teach public speaking, business, and entrepreneurship. Brendon made Keith realize that he had a message and great information to share.

Keith started a YouTube channel, where he talked about his landscaping business. He went for a very specific niche:

instead of just teaching homeowners how to take care of their yards, he focused on business owners. He wanted to teach people how to run their own landscaping companies.

He started shooting videos every single day. He has a great personality, a great sense of humor, and his authenticity shows through his videos. People are drawn to that. He knows how to deliver his message and sell it to his audience.

At first, Keith's family were not supportive of his new efforts. They literally held an intervention to try to get him to stop posting videos each day. It's sad, but sometimes the people closest to you can be dream killers. Be careful whom you share your hopes and dreams with. People sometimes won't see the point of what you're doing until after you've succeeded.

Keith didn't cut off his family and friends; he just ignored them. Now, on YouTube, he is the number-one result for almost any search related to landscaping and business. He has now expanded to shooting videos on how to start a window-washing business as well. Today Keith no longer lets the cold months stop him; he works out of a studio in his house. He focuses on producing videos, marketing, and selling his courses. This has allowed him to expand his ability to make an income online. His story exemplifies the movement of knowledge capital.

You can learn more about Keith Kalfas at Keith-Kalfas.MyKajabi.com.

### REMI BOUDREAU: COLOR SCHEME EXPERT

Remi was a successful house painter and contractor in Canada. He realized he had a knack for picking good paint schemes. He could see which colors went well together before he even started painting. Now he teaches professional house painters how to match colors and other aspects of business management.

Again, this is a great example of a niche within a niche. Instead of teaching people to paint their house, like many other YouTubers do, he focused specifically on how to pick a color scheme. If you search for him, you will see that he doesn't have videos to help homeowners. He specifically helps business owners.

I asked Remi if sharing all his secrets online negatively impacted his own painting business. Remi told me no, that sharing his knowledge has improved his own business. Now, instead of only reaching his one small part of Canada, he can impact people around the world.

Learn more about Remi's business at ExpressionsPaintingUniversity.com.

## INSIGHTS FROM THESE STORIES

Here are some things that I would really like you to think about when you remember the four individuals I've just discussed. You can also learn more about each of these entrepreneurs by visiting their websites, which are listed in the appendix.

### PEOPLE WANT TO KNOW WHAT YOU KNOW

If you've become an expert at something professionally, then you have the seeds of a potential business. There are so many skills you likely have obtained within your profession that you could share in some way. Think about how you can use information you already have.

### LOOK FOR A NARROWER NICHE

Also keep in mind that you may transform from one niche to another. I gave examples of people who had a specific niche. But when I began each story, you may have thought they would be selling one thing to a certain audience, and they ended up selling something different to a different audience than expected. They twisted the expectation to meet a specific need. For example, with Remi's story, it was not just about paint color. His niche is about how other painters can find the right colors. Really think about the unique angle you can take when you think about your niche.

## SHARE YOUR BEST STUFF FOR FREE

Remember that sharing free content can help develop a customer audience. You will need to get over the fear of giving away things for free, and in fact, you should give away your best stuff for free. People will feel a sense of reciprocity and want to give back to you, either by buying your stuff or by sharing with other potential customers. Once people know you, like you, and trust you, they will be more likely to buy from you.

Sharing knowledge does not have to negatively impact your profession. You do not have to hoard your knowledge out of a sense of competition. In fact, sharing your knowledge freely is what makes you stand out as an expert and allows potential customers to trust you.

## YOU CAN IMPROVE THE LIVES OF OTHERS

Finally, remember that your knowledge has the power to significantly improve other people's quality of life. I know a lot of you might be reading this, thinking, "I need to start a business to pay my bills or get out of this dead-end job," but that doesn't mean you can't change the world along the way.

## GUIDING QUESTIONS

Now that you've heard a few stories of people who turned

their professions into knowledge capital, it's time to turn the lens back on yourself. Get out a piece of paper and answer the following questions:

- Which of these journeys most inspired you and why?

- What is your current job?

- What jobs have you held in the past?

- What did you have to learn to do those jobs? Did you find it easy?

- What have people paid you for?

- What are you good at that people might pay you for but haven't yet?

- What do people frequently ask you to do or ask for your advice on? This can be outside of your job.

- In what ways does your profession contribute to your talents, vocation, and purpose? Think back to the purpose diagram.

# CHAPTER SIX

# PASSION AS KNOWLEDGE

In this chapter, I am going to cover stories of knowledge entrepreneurs whose knowledge derives from their personal interests and hobbies—what they love to do.

Many people believe that hobbies are just that—hobbies. But what if the thing you love to do in your free time could become your full-time job? That's what the people in the following stories have discovered, and their lives have ultimately improved because of it.

While you read through this chapter, think about the things that you are passionate about. Is there a business in there?

## TAMSEN HORTON: BUSINESS ATTORNEY TO BOSS MOM

Tamsen Horton is a Kajabi superfan, and her story is at the intersection of profession and passion.

She was a business attorney for years before she had kids. When her kids were born, she wanted to stay home with them while still contributing to the family financially. At first, she started using Skype to help other moms with legal issues. That was a great idea. She would literally turn on her laptop while holding one of her kids.

Another mom on the other side would say, "Hey, I've got this business and need to trademark this logo. What do I do?"

Tamsen would say, "No problem. I'll take care of it."

This is how she started making money from home.

The next step she took was to develop a course and start teaching what she had previously shared on Skype calls, only now with more people. That's when she fell in love with the idea of teaching online. This is where passion came in for her. What used to be her profession became her passion.

There is an important insight here, which we covered in

the last chapter. Tamsen recognized what others were asking her to do. In fact, she is probably one of the most fearless customers I have ever met. She never said, "Oh, that's not going to work. Should I do that? Should I be on camera?" No. She just did it. She has loved it from the start and her business has continued to expand.

As Tamsen continued her journey, she began to see other options. She didn't limit herself to only one topic. She now teaches other courses: one about parenting and one on how to write a book. She keeps trying more topics to see how they work. Recently, she told me that her husband, who is a teacher, launched his own online course during the summer.

Her example shows that if you set aside your fear, you might be surprised where it leads.

You can see all of Tamsen's courses at TamsenHorton.com.

## MICHELLE PARSLEY: ELEVATE YOUR ART

In this case, Michelle's passion is also her profession. She was a school photographer who took school portraits for a living. As a hobby, she did fine art photography. At some point, she entered and won a prestigious professional photographers' competition for the best photograph.

After winning, she became a judge. She saw other artists

struggling to win and not understanding the requirements. So she began coaching contestants. She ended up creating an entire course centered around how to prepare for photography competitions.

The crazy part is that there are only a few thousand people who would even want that course. It's a great example of targeting a small niche. You don't have to go after a huge audience. There is money to be made in small groups too. When I first heard Michelle's story, I was captivated by it because of her small unique niche and the angle she chose.

Today, she has a whole bunch of other courses. She has courses about how to take great photographs and how to edit with Photoshop to make them even better. But she started by only teaching about photography contests. Now she has a six-figure business and has built a whole empire around photography. She is a master photographer, artist, and coach. Her specialty is taking photographs and using Photoshop tools to make them look like paintings. Check out her work and courses at ElevateYourArt.com.

She is the perfect example of how any online business works. When you look at something she has done, you will likely think, "Wow, that's cool. How did she do that?" You will then Google to explore more, and there she will be, showing you how to do what she does.

## DIANE BLECK: DOODLE INSTITUTE

Diane's story is unique. She worked in a corporate setting, and part of her job was to do presentations that explained complicated concepts. Often people would use diagrams or long bulleted lists in their PowerPoint presentations, but Diane had another idea. She liked to doodle, and she decided to use doodles and symbols to help convey her ideas to clients.

When Diane was in school, doodling came much more naturally to her than note-taking. Once she started her job, her boss noticed her doodling and thought it was cool. She could take her skill of brainstorming and simplifying complex problems down to icons and sketches and turn that into her job. For a long time, she got paid good money to do just that.

Eventually, she realized, "I could teach other people how to do this. Maybe I could make more money teaching others." She began doing local seminars, and that is how she met Mike "Muddy" Schlegel. Muddy was a student who loved what she was doing so much that he wanted to work with her and take her message global. Together they founded the Doodle Institute.

The Doodle Institute doesn't just teach you how to draw. It teaches you how to unlock your creativity and become a better communicator via doodling. Diane also teaches an advanced course on how to build your own doodle-based business.

Can you believe it? We're talking about doodling here. When I was in school, my entire notepad was filled with doodles. I never had notes. I just doodled. I used to look down on myself for that. I would think, "Why can't I be a better student? Why can't I take better notes?" Imagine if the Doodle Institute had been around back then. I would have embraced it.

You might notice a theme here. Whether the niche is painting, mowing lawns, or doodling, those who have been most successful don't just teach others what to do. They teach others how to start a business around it. Not only is Diane teaching others creative communication by doodling, but she's also teaching people how to get work in that industry. And guess what? She's killing it. Her courses are blowing up. Check out her academy at DoodleInstitute.MyKajabi.com.

Diane is the perfect example of having a diamond right under your nose. Listen to that voice inside of you, let it guide you, and start following it. Don't just sit in that cubicle waiting for time to pass; start moving in the direction you want to go.

## JORDAN VALERIOTE: HARDCORE MUSIC STUDIO

For years, Jordan Valeriote played the guitar in different bands. Then he had the opportunity to get into production, and he fell in love with the process. He mixed hardcore rock music, and he worked as a music producer for seven years.

Eventually he realized he wanted other revenue streams. He had the idea to teach others his craft via one-on-one sessions. His belief was that he needed to charge a high price tag for lessons because he could only teach one student at a time. Unfortunately, nobody signed up.

Meanwhile, he had a Facebook page that had about 800 fans, and he thought, "Maybe I can find customers here." He created what is called a lead magnet. A lead magnet is something that you give away for free that attracts people and captures leads (usually email addresses). In Jordan's case, he used a free digital file of drum sounds. For people who mix music, this was very attractive, so they signed up.

Through his lead magnet, he collected about 300 email addresses. Then he did a video launch for his course, something we will discuss in Chapter Nine, and grew his list to 700 people. With the launch of his course, he immediately made $10,000.

Today his online business is extremely profitable. He also

expanded his sales using affiliates. Affiliates are people who refer Jordan's course to their own online audience for potential commission. This is a great way to grow your audience. He teaches hardcore rock music mixing, but he also receives references from others who teach jazz, drums, or voice.

Jordan's journey has been amazing—going from being in a garage band to using GarageBand to turn his knowledge into a career. You can find Jordan at HardcoreMusicStudio.com.

### FELICIA RICCI: BELT YOUR FACE OFF

As a kid, Felicia always wanted to be in musical theater, and she grew up to become a professional singer. Her biggest role to date has been as an understudy for Elphaba, the green witch in the Broadway musical *Wicked*.

Felicia wrote a book about her experience on Broadway called *Unnaturally Green: One Girl's Journey along a Yellow Brick Road Less Traveled*. To promote her memoir, she decided to start making YouTube videos. Her videos were about how to improve your singing voice, how to sing with more power, and other secrets she had learned about her talent.

Soon, the videos became very popular. One day, backstage, she was chatting with a coworker, and he told her about Kajabi and suggested she use her knowledge to create a course.

That was the nudge she needed: she decided to take her material and turn it into a video course. One of her courses is called Belt Your Face Off, which teaches you how to sing like a Broadway star. Felicia is currently a full-time singer, musician, and artist. While she no longer actively teaches singing, she has multiple online courses still available at FeliciaRicci.com.

## INSIGHTS FROM THESE STORIES

Here are the insights I would like you to digest after reading these stories. Again, you can learn more about each of these entrepreneurs by visiting their websites, which are listed in the appendix.

## KNOWLEDGE CAPITAL CAN BECOME A WAY OF LIFE

As you can see from these stories, a simple idea can turn into something life-changing. In many cases, these knowledge entrepreneurs made so much money they could quit their day jobs.

## YOUR PROFESSION CAN LEAD TO YOUR PASSION

You might start with a profession-based business and then grow from there with something that truly encompasses your passion. As we saw in Tamsen's story, she took what she knew as a business attorney and helped others with the knowledge she already had. Along the way, she realized her true passion was teaching and helping other people.

## A SMALL TARGET AUDIENCE IS A GOOD START

It's okay to start with a small audience to support your business. You can engage thousands of people or just a couple hundred people. If they are truly interested in what you are saying and willing to spend money to hear more, you will grow both your audience and your business.

## USE FREE CONTENT TO GROW YOUR EMAIL LIST

The final insight is to consider the importance of growing your customer list by providing customers with free content in exchange for their email address. Remember this is called a lead magnet.

Don't hoard your knowledge. Give away the best stuff you have because people will then want more knowledge from you. They will look forward to receiving more emails from you, and eventually trust you enough to buy from you.

## GUIDING QUESTIONS

Now that you've heard a few stories of people who turned their passions into knowledge capital, it's time to turn the lens back on yourself. The guiding questions below are also similar to the ones in the last chapter, but they are more geared to your passion rather than your profession.

Get out a piece of paper and answer the following questions:

- Which of these journeys most inspired you and why?

- What are your hobbies?

- What are your interests?

- What are the things you do in your free time?

- What sports are you good at or enjoy? You don't have to be good at the sport to find a viable business. Think back to my drone example.

- What do you do for free but would love to get paid for?

- What did you do as a child that you miss? Remember when we were kids and we would say, "When I grow up, I want to be this or that." Maybe you doodled in class, built things, sang, or threw a good curve ball. Those old talents should be clues for you.

- What is something you would do if you had more time?

- What energizes you? When you tap into your passion, you will now have that energy that you've been missing. If you can clear some other things from your life and find that knowledge niche, energy will come.

Finally, consider how the answers to all these questions have helped you further refine your knowledge niche. I hope that as you've been reading, you've experienced that nudging thought of "What if I did this?"

# CHAPTER SEVEN

# PAIN AS KNOWLEDGE

The stories I cover in this chapter will be about knowledge entrepreneurs who use their personal experience of physical, mental, or emotional pain to create knowledge products.

This chapter is about those experiences that almost debilitated us, overwhelmed us, set us back, or crushed us. I think all of us can relate to this, when something goes wrong in life and we don't know what to do—whether we experience back pain, debt, or divorce. I hope you can hear these stories and think about your own life.

Every one of these people dug deep and went to the root source of the pain. They first figured it out for themselves, and then they started sharing their experiences with other people. Sharing their experiences with others helped give their struggle meaning. Maybe what they went through had a purpose after all. Eventually, sharing their pain turned into a full-time business. It's really exciting to see the journey these entrepreneurs went on.

## SHANE DOWD: GOT ROM

Shane was a strength and conditioning coach at a CrossFit gym. He would coach people to work harder, lift more weight, and push themselves to the limit. One day, he was doing some heavy lifting. On the third set, something started to feel wrong in his back. When he put down the weights, he couldn't straighten back up and he knew something was very wrong.

For a month, he was in such pain that he needed his girlfriend to help him put on socks. Eventually he was diagnosed with Femoroacetabular Impingement, or FAI, and his doctors said he needed surgery. At this point, Shane was only in his midtwenties, so to think he already needed hip surgery was crazy. He thought there had to be another way to heal himself, and opted out of surgery.

He started doing a lot of research. He would search, "What can I do to get rid of this pain?" He was obsessed with finding answers.

He got into yoga, he tried deep tissue massages, met with

chiropractors, and stretched every day. Shane was truly on a mission to figure this out. In the meantime, he was still trying to train people. In a way, he experimented on himself and his clients until he was an expert about range of motion. After some time, he got past his pain, and it finally went away.

His initial diagnosis of FAI was very serious and the condition caused him tremendous back pain. Imagine how Shane felt after he heard the doctors tell him he needed surgery. I'm sure he felt lost, scared, and afraid. This painful experience could have changed him negatively, but instead, because of his commitment to finding the source of his pain, he found a solution.

Today, Shane is using his experiences to teach others how to prevent this type and other types of injuries at the gym. Now he is one of the best range-of-motion experts out there who knows how to fix this issue. If you search "fix FAI" on Google, he is the number-one result. He teaches online courses through his site, GotROM.com, where he even shares the video of the lift where he injured himself. Shane also shows how his flexibility has completely changed and how his new range of motion has allowed him to do so much more, including the splits. Check out Shane's courses at GotROM.com.

Think about your own life. Has there been an injury in

your life? Have you faced surgery, disease, or a situation that was extremely difficult? Did you go deeper and figure out a solution for yourself first? Maybe you can find your purpose by sharing your experiences and your knowledge to give back and help other people.

## ELISSA WEINZIMMER: VOICE BODY CONNECTION

Growing up, Elissa was a theater kid. She always wanted to do musical theater. She would perform for her family. She would get her brothers and sisters together and put on plays. Elissa pursued this passion all the way to the University of Southern California, where she majored in performing arts.

She was doing extremely well until she got to her last year of college. Knowing she only had a few months left of school, she started drinking a little more and staying out a bit later. She continued to push herself to do extremely well in her program, but eventually, the partying caught up with her, and she had a complete vocal breakdown.

The doctor explained she had a vocal hemorrhage with acid reflux. The combination of pushing herself with the lifestyle of drinking made her vocal cords bleed. That was it for her. She lost her voice, and she was not allowed to talk for a month. She could only write down messages.

Imagine how she felt; her whole life she'd pursued a dream until she hit this major tragedy, this roadblock that said to her, "Stop; go in a different direction."

Elissa did what a lot of successful Kajabi customers have done at some point along their journeys. She asked, "How can I fix this for myself?"

At first, she stopped performing. She was afraid to have her vocal cords fail again because she remembered how terrible it felt. She decided to pursue other areas of performing, like directing. But in the meantime, she was researching everything she could about voice, the body, and how the body and voice can heal.

She took everything she found and turned it into a course called Voice Body Connection. She teaches how the voice works and how to use it more effectively. She took the pain of losing her voice and the possibility of losing her dreams, and she worked backwards. She thought, "What could I have done differently? What did I do wrong? How could I have avoided this, and how can I get the most out of my voice?"

As she went through her own personal process, she thought, "Somebody should have shown me all of this. Someone should have taught me how to prep my voice or what you're supposed to do to sing louder. Someone should have taught me how to have more longevity with my voice."

These questions in her head sparked an idea. She decided that she would start teaching others what she wasn't taught. She researched more and more, and eventually, she had the perfect idea for a niche.

When she first got started, she would also ask her customers questions, like "What is the one thing you wish you knew about your voice?" Then she would use that information. She would research it and figure out new solutions for pains she hadn't even experienced. Through this process, Elissa expanded her knowledge and then chose to share what she had learned with her customers. On VoiceBodyConnection.com she now offers online classes, workshops, and private coaching to help people learn how to have a powerful and strong voice. Her story is a great example of how to become an expert within a niche.

## DY ANN PARHAM: AGING WITH GRACE

Dy Ann became a fitness fanatic after having kids. She lived a very healthy lifestyle by eating healthy, counting calories, and following meal plans. Once she turned fifty, she felt her hormones were changing and so was her body. Her mood was off, she had insomnia, and she started to gain weight. She tried her normal routine of cutting calories and following a strict diet plan, but nothing was working. The real shocker was when her doctor told her that she was prediabetic and was showing signs of a failing thyroid. Someone suggested that she try intermittent fasting.

Intermittent fasting is when you choose to consume your calories only during a specific window of time during the day. It's a patterned way of eating. For example, you only eat between 10 a.m. and 6 p.m. After 6 p.m. you are not allowed to eat again until the next day at 10 a.m.

Dy Ann started researching the subject. When she went online, she realized that most of the information available was for weight lifters or models trying to lose all their body fat. She couldn't find anything that was relevant to what women her age were going through or what she was going through.

She tested a lot of different things to see what would work for her. Soon, she started seeing results. Next, she made a Facebook group and contacted everybody she knew. She said, "Here is what I've been doing. I have been doing this intermittent fasting and getting these results. I have lost weight. My mood is better. And I have more energy. It has completely changed my life, and I want to start sharing what I have learned with others. If you'd like to learn more, join my Facebook group." She told people, "Give me twenty dollars. If it doesn't work for you, I will give you the twenty dollars back." She was basically testing out the concept to see if anyone would pay.

She started helping a bunch of people and realized, "I need to put more information out there." She started making a video every single weekday. She also does live video sometimes. For her, it is all about capturing her journey: "Here is what I've gone through. Here's what I've done. Here's what worked and didn't work. Here's what you could try."

Through doing this, she created quite a following.

Now Dy Ann offers online courses about intermittent fasting for her target audience. She also offers coaching and nutrition advice. She created an entire business around solving her almost debilitating health issues. The issues were starting to change her lifestyle, until she realized there was another lifestyle she could switch over to.

She explains how intermittent fasting really changed her life. Her online business allows her to schedule out her week and do things that really matter.

Connect with Dy Ann at DyAnnParham.com.

## MATT CODDE: OCD ACADEMY

Matt suffers from obsessive-compulsive disorder (OCD). He was diagnosed in his younger years and struggled with it throughout his young adult life. After college, when he became a social worker in Orange County, he saw a lot of people who struggled with the same disorder. He didn't know how to help them, and there really wasn't anything out there in terms of resources. Frustrated, he decided to start documenting what he personally was doing to overcome OCD.

He started making YouTube videos to share information and techniques he had used when dealing with his OCD. At first, he just put all the information out there, and then he packed it all together and put it into a course. For him, it was all about helping others. At the same time, it was financially rewarding. Today, people who are looking for valuable resources regarding OCD can find them at OCDAcademy.com.

This is a great example of someone who focused on a topic most people don't talk about. On the internet, where people feel they should be perfect, Matt was talking about a real pain. His knowledge became helpful and powerful.

After he started his course, Matt became a Kajabi hero—meaning he made over $1,000 and had some success. He loved what Kajabi did for his life and his customers, so he later reached out to us here at Kajabi and asked to come work with us. At the time of writing this book, Matt now works on our marketing team and is an incredible member of Kajabi. He is both a team member and a customer who really understands the struggle people go through when they want to take their knowledge and turn it into a business.

## INSIGHTS FROM THESE STORIES

### IF A STRATEGY WORKED FOR YOU, IT CAN ALSO HELP OTHERS

If a strategy, technique, or fix worked for you to overcome your pain or suffering, it will likely benefit others as well. As you have seen in these stories, each person overcame something and then started sharing their knowledge. Some of these people didn't even have an idea or plan for a business. They just wanted to share what they had learned and continue to learn for themselves. Eventually, others benefited, and the result became a business. A knowledge capital business.

### TEST YOUR IDEA WITH A SMALL COMMUNITY FIRST

Could you test your idea with a small community first and grow from there? Could you create a Facebook group like Dy Ann did? Could you text a group of friends and say, "Hey, is anyone else struggling with this? This is what happened to me, this is what I found, and this is what is working." When you are focused on helping others and not trying to sell something like a multilevel marketing or a get-rich-quick scheme, you might be surprised by how many people will say, "I have that same problem. Let me try this out."

Remember the importance of being real. When you're unauthentic and fake about the pains you have faced, people will sense that. But when you are real and honest and have genuine empathy, you can really make an impact on people's lives.

## KNOWLEDGE CAPITAL CAN BE A PLATFORM TO REACH YOUR COMMUNITY

There is power in being able to create a safe place, where you can talk about your pain and how you overcame it. That starts the dialogue, and then you can reach new communities of people you didn't know how to reach. I hope that through a story like Shane's, you can see how you could be able to help more people than you know.

## YOUR EXPERIENCE CAN HELP OTHERS WITH THEIR PAIN

When you encountered a pain or struggle in life, you

decided to find a solution. Once you succeeded in dealing with this problem or difficulty, hopefully you decided that your knowledge could help others. This is what we call a hero's journey. You first became the hero of your own life, and now you will become the hero of other people's lives.

Many of us don't think we are heroic. We don't think we can do this. But you would be surprised by the power that's already inside you. That remarkable knowledge that you gained by going through those painful experiences, that is something that you need to share with the world, especially if you're reading this book.

If you're starting to feel like "I could do this," it's important to listen to that voice. You probably have been ignoring it your whole life. All of us have done this. I know I used to ignore all my gifts and blessings, but now I use them to help other people.

## GUIDING QUESTIONS

Now that you've heard a few stories of people who turned their personal pain into knowledge capital, it's time to turn the lens back on yourself.

You need to listen to that voice inside of you. It is speaking a message of purpose. It will only be able to give you clues. If you have never done this before, the clues will seem very subtle, which is why we tend to ignore them. But don't ignore them, they are trying to tell you something and nudge you in the right direction.

Get out a piece of paper and answer the following questions:

- Which of these stories most inspired you, and why?

- Have you ever experienced considerable physical, mental, or emotional pain?

- Have you overcome something devastating?

- Did you learn or develop tools or strategies to help manage or overcome your pain?

- Do you know a home remedy that works? For example, when you get a headache or have back pain, what do you do? Is there a home remedy among your family or friends that you have used? Has it worked? Start paying attention.

- Do you ever get asked how you overcame something or managed something?

- How does your pain or conquering of pain affect your purpose?

I have hinted at this a lot: I think we're all looking for purpose in our lives. Everybody talks about this on the internet. If you're religious, people talk about it at church all the time. I certainly believe that God, the creator, put a gift inside each and every one of us, and our life's purpose is to unwrap that gift and share it with the world. The sad part is that many people never discover their gift. Or they never have the courage to share it. They just go about their lives with their heads down, only focusing on the next step in their lives. Now is your opportunity to dig deep, discover your gift, and look for your real purpose.

It's not just about starting a business, it's about changing people's lives and making a difference. The money part is just a bonus. When you are finally doing what you love and are getting paid for it, this is a win for both you and your customer. Look back to the purpose diagram in Chapter Four. This is that diagram in action. I hope the stories are inspiring you to consider how this could happen to you too.

# CHAPTER EIGHT

# PROBLEMS AS KNOWLEDGE

The stories covered in this chapter are about knowledge entrepreneurs whose knowledge products derive from their experiences of figuring out and solving a problem.

In the last chapter, we talked about pain. Pain and problems are very similar, and sometimes they cross over. It doesn't really matter if the source of knowledge is from pain or a problem, but I put them in separate categories to hopefully help you better identify sources of knowledge in your life. Typically, a problem is associated with an area in which you feel stuck and don't know what to do. You need to figure it out. Pain is something that physically or emotionally hurts.

## JEANNE KELLY: CREDIT COACH

When Jeanne Kelly went through a divorce, it completely trashed her credit. She was a single mom with a young daughter, and she didn't even have enough credit to rent an apartment. She worked as a waitress and endured many sleepless nights. It took her over three years to unravel her credit issues and begin to fix them.

After she figured out how to fix her own credit, she realized she wanted to help others do the same. It made her feel good. However, she was a single mom and crazy involved in her daughter's life. She was also still working hard to pay the bills.

She started a small credit repair business called the Kelly Group. Back in 2000, it was just her, but she liked the idea of calling her business the Kelly Group because it made it sound like a bigger company, even though she had no experience and no customers.

This was all before social media. You may be worried about finding customers, and I will show you ways to get them later in this book. But imagine how Jeanne felt. She didn't have Facebook or Instagram or even a way to connect to the internet. How would you find customers if you were in her shoes?

Well, she found customers the old-fashioned way. She pulled

out the yellow pages and found mortgage companies. Her idea was that people want to fix their credit so that they can qualify for loans or get better rates. She thought there had to be mortgage bankers out there looking for somebody like her. She literally went door to door, knocking and talking to anyone who would open the door. For a long time, she heard a lot of nos. No after no after no. Finally, one mortgage broker said, "Sure, can you fix this customer's credit?"

After that first customer, she started doing one-on-one coaching with more customers. Then she started doing public speaking. She really got out there and made a name for herself. One day, CNN contacted her for a quote in an article. Then the *New York Times* called and asked her to do the same thing. Suddenly, Jeanne Kelly became a nationally known credit expert.

Imagine, this single mom who was working as a waitress with no money and no credit was having trouble finding a place to live, and spent three years fixing her credit problem. But she didn't stop there, she was brave enough to share her knowledge. She kept knocking on doors until she got a connection. Then big news outlets reached out to her because her message was out there. Before she knew it, Jeanne had plenty of customers and has now been in business for over seventeen years.

In the last couple years, Jeanne realized what she was

teaching was important for everybody—not just people buying houses or people who had money, but anyone who had bad credit. She wanted to help more people, so she decided to put her information online. She shot videos and explained what to do. She put her entire message that she had been crafting for years into an online course. Now she reaches people all over the world. People come to her, and she loves it. She said, "It's so fulfilling to know that I am reaching people everywhere."

The fact that she can do all this online means she can do one-on-one coaching with people all over the world right from her home. You can learn more about Jeanne by visiting her website at JeanneKelly.net.

## KENDRA WRIGHT: THE YEAR OF FEAR

Kendra always wanted to be a writer. She wanted to start a blog, but she was afraid. The fear held her back. She thought, "What if I write something and people are super critical of me or say I don't know anything or don't like what I write about?

I am sure you've probably felt this kind of fear before. If you are already thinking about creating a knowledge capital business, this thought has likely crept into your head: "Who is going to listen to me?" Don't worry, Kendra had the same fear.

She finally summoned the courage to put up her first blog post on HeyKendra.com and decided to face her fears head on. She emailed every single person she was afraid of judging her and sent them her post.

How about that for overcoming your fear? Kendra decided to go right for it. That's when she realized that there were a lot of things she had been avoiding because of fear, so she challenged herself to start doing scary things. Eventually, she started facing more fears and posting on social media about what she was doing to get out of her comfort zone.

She dubbed 2013 the Year of Fear. She decided that every single day, she would do something to get out of her comfort zone. She told me, "When you follow the things you love and do what is difficult, weird magic happens."

She did all sorts of things. She went on police ride-alongs. She picked up hitchhikers and made friends with three incredible Canadians who were traveling across her area. She went to a retirement home and asked to speak to the loneliest person there. She ended up spending an evening with a ninety-eight-year-old woman she never would have met otherwise.

One piece of advice Kendra gives her readers is to start challenging themselves with one simple action. For example, try to take a different route on the way home one night. It's an easy challenge to do something different. It's not always about something being scary; sometimes we stay stuck simply because we keep doing the same thing. Get outside the norm; don't let yourself be stuck in a rut or the same habit. Who knows what you might find on the other side?

After Kendra was deep into her journey, she knew she wanted to use her platform to teach others about ways to overcome fear and embrace change. Her experience had been incredible, and she wanted to share and help others do the same. So she created her course called Facing Fear.

The first person she told this idea to was skeptical and asked her, "Who would pay for that?" The amazing part of the story is that the same person who questioned her idea eventually ended up buying and doing her course. He thought it was great. You should understand that this experience might happen to you too. Whether you want to teach people about credit, weight loss, horseback riding, or whatever it is, someone will say, "No, no. You can't, you can't."

But let me tell you, if you have gone through a problem, there are people on the other side who want your solutions, your guidance, and your expertise. In the coming chapters, we are going to talk about creating your knowledge capital project. If you can find these people who are looking for what you have to share, there is a product there too.

## ADAM JORDAN: TEXTING PRINCE

Adam Jordan is now the Texting Prince, but he started his career as a second-grade teacher. He enjoyed teaching kids, but he knew there was something more he needed to do with his life.

In college, Adam had struggled with dating, so he studied confidence techniques. The techniques Adam learned helped him get dates. He got so many dates that, eventually, his friends started asking him for dating advice.

In the age of Tinder and smartphones, a lot of dating revolves around texting. Unfortunately, a lot of people aren't very good at the written word. But Adam had a real knack for using texts to create amazing conversations with people. Adam seemed to know exactly what to say, and his friends could see that. Eventually, Adam's friends suggested that he should share his knowledge more widely.

They told him, "You need to do a course on text dating and how to text to get dates."

He said, "No, no, I don't want to do that. No way."

Some of you may relate to Adam's experience. Perhaps those around you have told you that you are really good at something. They say, "That thing you told me...well, it totally worked." Don't ignore that. Listen to that voice.

Listen to those clues that are happening to you. If you don't, you will keep hearing it. That voice will keep coming back because it's trying to nudge you in the right direction.

Adam's friends kept pushing, and he kept saying no. But he still heard that small voice inside of him telling him that he needed to help others. At last, he went for it. He started making simple courses on how to text, what to say, and all the techniques for interacting with someone you're trying to date. And it worked. Adam is now considered the Texting Prince, and you can find him at TextingPrince.com. His online courses include Texting Master, Swipe Right, and Setting a Date Over Texting. He now teaches all kinds of people his texting techniques. He loves guiding others who have the same dating problems he once had.

### SHANNON O'BRIEN: ISUGAR UNIVERSITY

Shannon is a licensed aesthetician who originally owned a spa near Lake Tahoe, California. She specialized in facials and waxing. Shannon had two young boys and wanted to find better schools for them. So she sold her day spa and moved to Sacramento.

Around this time, the recession hit. Suddenly people didn't have a lot of disposable income for facials, and her business started to struggle. One day after work, Shannon was at a happy hour, and she overheard a couple of ladies talking about getting "sugared." She was curious, so she did some research.

Sugar hair removal is a way to remove body hair using only water, lemon, and sugar. The mixture is simple and nontoxic. It's literally edible, although Shannon doesn't recommend sampling it after it's been used. It's a very clean and organic procedure.

Shannon saw an opportunity. Hair removal is something people don't give up, even during a recession. They might not go as often, but they will still go to get "sugared." She thought, "I'm going to learn how to do this."

She started doing sugaring and she became very popular. People love it because it is less painful and nontoxic. Soon, the sugaring supply companies asked if they could send a couple people out to get trained by her. She would close her entire shop for an afternoon to train two or three people and make a little side money.

After a while, she thought, "There's got to be a way for me to put this online." Now Shannon has been sharing her knowledge online for seven years. She used the original version of Kajabi and started teaching everything she knew when she got certified herself.

It's funny to hear her journey of promoting her teachings

online. She tried using Periscope, an app that allows you to go live and talk about a subject on video, and people in your area can find you. She would go live and talk about waxing and other relevant topics, like bikini wax, Brazilian wax, and anything relevant. The most random people would show up on her feed and watch her discuss these topics. She also connected with a lot of people who would say, "Oh my gosh. This is really cool."

Now Shannon calls herself the Sugar Mama. She is an expert in her field and is well-known around the world. Big beauty companies send people to her iSugar University online course to become certified sugar technicians. With her new online course and certification process, she's able to impact the entire industry.

She has taken a topic that was kind of secretive, that we all laugh about, and she has fully embraced it. Shannon uses her funny personality to develop her online brand. She is just her authentic self, and it has worked for her. Now she says, "I never would have thought my business would have turned into this, but it has, and I love it."

### INSIGHTS FROM THESE STORIES
KNOWLEDGE CAPITAL CAN BE TRANSFORMATIVE FOR YOUR AUDIENCE AND YOU

Consider the last story, about Shannon. Not only was she

able to help her customers and build her business, but how amazing is it that she was also able to become an influencer in her industry?

What is the industry you work in? Have you made any innovations or solved any problems? Maybe you could influence your entire industry with your unique knowledge. You might be able to become the one go-to person doing something you haven't even considered.

## AN ACCOUNTABILITY PARTNER CAN HELP YOU

Consider finding an accountability partner to help support and develop the creation of You, Inc.

Remember Kendra and the negative words that were said to her? Well, throughout the process of doing her "Year of Fear," she also had accountability partners. They would reach out to her regularly to see how she was doing or see if she needed anything. Perhaps you can enlist someone else to read this book with you or have someone you trust encourage you to follow this dream. Be accountability partners for each other as you move through these steps to take your knowledge and turn it into a business.

## THE PROBLEM THAT FUELS YOUR BUSINESS COULD BE BIG AND FUNDAMENTAL...OR NARROW AND LIMITED

You don't need to be an expert in everything; you just need to be good at one thing. When most of us think about business, we want to have something big right away, but small is actually a great way to start. Your personality, your experience, and your knowledge can make an impact in a small industry very quickly.

The problem that ends up sparking the idea for your knowledge capital business can be fundamental to who you are, or it may be limited to a certain area of your life. Maybe as you read these stories and dig deep, you can remember a problem that you've found a solution for.

## DON'T BE DISCOURAGED IF OTHERS ARE ALREADY OUT THERE

The first thing people will tell you is that "someone else already did that." Take for example, Jeanne, the credit lady. Sure, there are other people in that sphere that teach about credit and paying off debt. But it was her personality, her story, and her perseverance that attracted her audience.

What makes this all work is the power of *you*. There is no other you. You are the secret recipe to your online business.

## GUIDING QUESTIONS

Now that you've heard a few stories of people who turned their problems into knowledge capital businesses, it's time to turn the lens back on yourself.

Get out a piece of paper and answer the following questions:

- Which of these stories most inspired you and why?

- What major problems, mistakes, or obstacles have you conquered or overcome?

- What makes you imperfect? Your struggle sometimes will show you what your gift is. Kendra's story is a great example of the struggle of fear. By moving toward her fear, she became an expert on overcoming fear.

- Did something ever happen to you that you wish hadn't?

- How does your experience of overcoming a problem, mistake, or obstacle refine your purpose?

# PART THREE

# LAUNCHING YOU, INC.

# CHAPTER NINE

# DETERMINE YOUR KNOWLEDGE PRODUCT

By now you've seen over a dozen examples of entrepreneurs who used their special talents and knowledge to create their own businesses. You hopefully have some ideas about your own unique expertise. In this chapter, I'm going to go one step further by guiding you through some strategies for developing your own knowledge-based product.

But first, one more story.

## ZACH SPUCKLER: HEART, SOUL, AND HUSTLE

Since Zach was thirteen, he has been making money online. He was always selling, marketing, and doing all kinds of cool stuff. He always had something going on in the background, even as he went to school.

By the time he reached grad school, Zach had a mountain of student loan debt. He was exhausted all the time from working, going to school, and staying up all night to hack together his online businesses which he was able to scale to a level that allowed him to leave school and pursue his business full time.

Today he makes six figures by taking what he learned about online marketing and teaching other people to do product launches and what he calls "five-day challenges." He has fully embraced his online business.

Instead of taking the path that was expected of him, he said, "I'm not going to do it." I think it's important that you get to this point. Your mind must be open. You may have to make some changes that seem to go against how you were raised, how you understood the economy to work, or how you saw the world. This is the time to allow your mind to shift.

Now that you understand what is possible and have started to figure out your knowledge niche, how do you get started? The next step is to consider possible sellable products tied to your profession, passion, pain, problems, or purpose.

I am going to use what I like to call the "You, Inc. Formula" of your niche—people, product, and profit. You need all three for these to work.

## PEOPLE: FIND YOUR TRIBE

First, what do I mean by people? These are going to be your end users who care about your profession, passion, pain, or problem—these are your customers, or what some people call your tribe.

What have you overcome? What have you solved? What have you fixed? Start with yourself. You have a certain skill or passion. You have overcome a certain problem. Now it's about finding the other *yous* out there.

In all the examples we've talked about, each business owner started out as someone just looking for answers. They did the research, figured things out, and then shared their knowledge with others who had similar questions. People who need those same answers that you researched: Are they out there? Do they exist? Or are you the only one?

There are some topics that are so obscure that it can be difficult to find a paying audience. At the end of all of this, it's not just about helping people. It's about changing your life, which means you must find a way to turn the topic into a business, which means you must find an audience. So are there people out there like you? Most likely there are.

You can start with your circle of friends and family. Remember Dy Ann Parham? She started by putting her experience with intermittent fasting on Facebook. She literally contacted friends and family and said, "Hey, I've done this. I've had these results. Who out there is interested?"

That can be scary. For every ten people you contact, one or two will be negative or critical. They will say, "Nah, why would you do that?" Remember Kendra's story? The first person she told her idea to said, "Who's going to pay you for that?" Try not to let those people deter you from your path. Learn to ignore them and just keep going. Trust me, the people who laughed at you at the beginning will be buying your course and raving about it at the end.

The next thing you need to do is find your tribe. These are the people who want what you are offering. I say this is your tribe because they will gather. As someone who has been through this thing, you will become their leader, guiding them forward. They will listen when you say, "Hey guys, I tried this. It worked." You also must be willing to say, "I did this, and it failed." When a group of people come together around a subject and find openness and honesty about the ups and downs, that is where the magic happens.

As a leader, people are looking to you for guidance. Do not get overwhelmed; remember you only really need to be an expert at this one thing. Think about Elissa from Mind Body Connection. She became an expert in voice coaching by specifically researching voice trauma issues. It's important to stay focused in your niche. Once you get down to the point of specificity, you can become the expert and become the person that people turn to.

Your people, your audience, are likely right under your nose, and you don't even realize it. You are interacting with them all the time, and you don't even know it. Think about that. What YouTube videos do you watch? Who are the people making comments on those videos? When you're on Facebook, what do you comment on? What do you post on social media? What if you switched what you were posting slightly and focused a bit more on your niche? I bet you would start finding your tribe.

## START SMALL

With some of the examples I have given, the audience numbers have not been big. Please don't think that you need a million followers to start. Trust me, it doesn't need to be a big number. You can easily start with one thousand people, one hundred people, or even ten people in a Facebook group. Some things are a lot more lucrative when they are smaller. A smaller number could mean more authenticity in your audience. It could also make it easier for you to connect with your tribe.

Again, the number of people doesn't matter, but you do need to start with people. Remember Michelle Parsley from ElevateYourArt.com in Chapter Six? She only had five thousand potential customers with her first course, and today she's making six figures doing what she does. It wasn't like she was going after all photographers or photography business owners. She was going after a small group of people.

The cool thing about Michelle's story is that she started with that one product, became an expert, and made money. From that course, she could branch out to other products that are relevant for her audience. The more knowledge she shares, the more she attracts people with the same interests, which then allows her to broaden her market even more.

## PITFALLS TO AVOID

Beware of wanting to merely create awareness. Awareness is a good thing. It's great for people to be aware about healthy eating, taking care of the environment, or best ways to raise their kids. We need to talk about these things. We should always question ourselves and continually grow. But awareness alone doesn't necessarily lead to a business.

Consider Shannon, the Sugar Mama. She didn't just stick to creating awareness that sugaring was a nontoxic, organic, and safe method of hair removal. She took it a step further and created a course with a certification program. You can then create as much awareness as you want, but you should first make sure there is money there, that capital is in there somewhere.

Don't just show people how to do something simple. Try to cater your knowledge and message to people who can help make you money. Oftentimes this means other business owners. For example, take Nicole Begley, the pet photographer. She doesn't just teach people how to take photos of their pets. Nicole took it a step further and created a course on how to start your own pet photography business.

Another great example of someone who did this is Greg Todd of GregToddTV.com. He is a physical therapist who targets other physical therapy business owners rather than just the masses. Rather than just teaching patients how to overcome their pain or do certain exercises, he helps physical therapists to be great at their business. That has become his niche of customers. The key here is that as you are trying to find people who will pay you money for your product, don't try to reach everybody. You just need to reach the right people.

Another common mistake is to define your niche too

broadly. When you narrow down your expertise to its strongest subcategory, you also narrow down your target audience to the people who will be the most interested. Again, I like to use the example of golfing. Instead of going after all golfers, why not narrow it down to just left-handed golfing? Or how to get out of sand traps? Or how to drive a golf ball three hundred yards?

## TARGETING YOUR NICHE

Here are a few sources for identifying possible niches.

### Amazon

Start searching Amazon for your category or topic and see what pops up. Has anybody written about this? Are there magazines that cover this topic? Is there a category of books or a subcategory within Amazon that deals with this?

### Magazines

You might be shocked to hear this, but there are still magazines around. Go into any book store, and you will find a myriad of magazines covering every conceivable topic, from space aliens to guns, and from pets to poker. If there is a magazine dealing with your niche, then you have a bit of a head start. You can easily start doing research on your target audience here.

## YouTube

YouTube is one of the biggest research tools there is. See what other people are saying about your topic. Most people on YouTube are not monetizing their knowledge correctly. Most don't even get it. They just want fifteen minutes of fame and some ad revenue. They don't realize the possibilities. You can't make much money on YouTube with that strategy, but if you build a brand and platform, you can build an online empire.

## Podcasts

If you're not a podcast person, I encourage you to start listening to them. They are free, and you can get them right on your smartphone. Get on there. Listen to podcasts. When you're driving or working out, it's a great way to listen to content. Is there a podcast about your niche? If there is, see what that person is doing. They may be a potential partner for you. You never know.

As you begin to research, don't get discouraged if someone is already covering the same topic. It will be rare for you to find a topic that is not covered. At this point, the internet evolves and grows at its own pace. It is its own entity, its own brain, and almost every area and topic has been touched or covered.

Think about it this way. If someone is already in your space, then you know there is a market for it. People are already trying and testing it. There's already a community, and you can go study it. You need to find something unique to offer in that same space. Remember that You, Inc. is about *you*. This will be your personality, your character, your humor, your mistakes, your unique way of overcoming something. That is what makes your brand.

*You* are the real capital of this knowledge, *you* are the brand, and that is what will sell and build your business.

## PRODUCT: SELLING YOURSELF

Developing a product is where you turn your expertise into something that can be packaged and sold.

The first product you will need to work on is your own personal brand. You are the expert, and therefore, you are the product. Your sellable product starts with you and your chosen topic. Think about what you need to know, how you rose above a challenge, or how you overcame a problem when you were in your customer's position. Go back to solving that problem.

Start with your name. Some people keep their name. Their brand is Greg Todd or Jeanne Kelly. Others use a nickname like the Sugar Mama or the Texting Prince. Either way, you must start branding yourself.

Kenny Keller is a knowledge entrepreneur who teaches helicopter flying. He is a good example of someone who packaged their knowledge into a sellable product. Kenny found that passing the helicopter flight test was very difficult. Beyond just knowing how to fly, you are required to do Ground School, which involves hours of training and studying.

Kenny took everything he did to pass the test and made a giant notebook. He turned all his notes into a study guide, which became his sellable product. He began selling it on Amazon.

When Kenny thought back to his own struggle to become a helicopter pilot, he saw a real problem, a need. He took the knowledge he had and put it into this downloadable product. Eventually, he also made content that people could listen to or watch. He made himself an expert in the field. He first solved the problem for himself and then created an online helicopter-flight-training empire. You can find Kenny Keller on HelicopterGround.com.

### KEEP IT SIMPLE

Your product does not need to be complex. Most of the examples in this book started very organically. Oftentimes people started with just a sharable PDF that people were willing to pay for. You could write about the ten steps to fix your credit, for example. Maybe that resource guide is over a hundred pages and you sell that.

Remember the Beanie Baby craze in the 1990s? Rick Steele is an online entrepreneur who used to sell Beanie Babies on eBay. He made a lot of money, and along the way, he made up a guide for all the Beanie Babies—showing how much they cost and where to buy them. He did this just to keep his business organized. Then he thought, "What if I sell this guide?" It was like a big directory. Seriously, it was like the Kelly Blue Book for Beanie Babies. That business took off more than selling the Beanie Babies.

Other types of products you can sell are short videos or audio guides. Today, videos are super easy to make. You can just take an iPhone video or shoot a video on your home computer.

Another kind of content is any downloadable file. Remember Jon, the Excel expert? He offered digital content downloads of his training and his program files. For those of you who have jobs on the computer and are experts at a program, what if you could sell a digital file? Maybe you could sell it as training—how to make a Photoshop flyer or how Excel can help you budget your money. Or you could sell the actual file, like a music file. Remember Jordan, from HardcoreMusicStudio.com, who started by giving away the drum sounds? If you have ever played with music online, it's just a series of files for different sounds. As a hardcore rocker, music mixer, and producer, Jordan had access to these files and just gave them away.

Keep in mind that your product offerings can evolve over time. Develop an online course and then respond to the needs or interests of your audience with other products. Elissa, who did the voice training course, would ask customers, "What else do you want to know about your voice? What else do you want to know about your body and singing?" She used that knowledge to evolve her products over time.

Your first product does not need to be perfect either. You just need to get something out there and make iterations as you go. Get it out there and test the reaction. You will get feedback, but you can't fail if you don't give up. If you put something out and it sucks and nobody likes it, you only fail if you stop. But if you ask them why they don't like it, you can improve it; you can do it again and be on your way. Give yourself grace. You are still just getting started with this. Nobody is perfect right out of the gate.

## PROFIT

Profit is an essential third ingredient of the You, Inc. Formula. All three are important, but this last one is crucial. If you can't make a product that results in profit, the formula will not work.

In so many of the stories I have shared, the person started by making their first hundred, then they made a thousand, and then ten thousand. Now some of them have even become millionaires. Imagine that life. Imagine customers paying you for your knowledge as your business grows.

It's essential that the people in your market are willing to pay for your product. Not everyone will, but there is usually a subset of your tribe who will be willing to pay. Who are they? Where are they?

You should first do the research to make sure people are willing to pay for your product. If people are talking about your topic, there is a good chance they would be willing to pay for your product. Start with a lower-priced product and increase the price as you incrementally improve. Maybe you start with offering something for ten dollars. Maybe your first offer is free videos, just to get the content out there and test the market. See if people are interested.

You can often find where the profits are by approaching things from a different angle. Remember Remi Boudreau, the paint-matching expert from Canada? Even though there are more homeowners than professional painters, he went after the minority. He narrowed his audience. It might seem like the logical thing to do is go for the big audience, but homeowners might not be willing to pay for advice on choosing paint. When Remi went after professional painters with his knowledge, helping them be better at their jobs, they saw value there because they could expand their business. Think about how you could narrow your market to people who are willing to pay you for it. Is there a business tied to your knowledge? Do you know something that could help people in that business?

Another example is the doodle expert, Diane Bleck. She was great at drawing pictures to explain complex things. She took that random hobby, that random thing she had gotten in trouble for at school, and realized business owners could benefit from it. Then she took it a step further, and she showed people how they could build a business as doodling consultants.

## ESTABLISHING A PRICE POINT

Here are a few guidelines for establishing an initial price for your product.

You may be surprised that people right now are charging $99, $1,000, or even $10,000 for knowledge products. How could anybody do that? Well, think about it. Have you gone to college? How much does it typically cost for one class? Often one class costs thousands of dollars. A class at a community college might be cheaper, but it is still hundreds of dollars. Imagine the impact your content could have on someone's life. What is it worth?

If you already have some people in your tribe, ask them how much they would pay you for your product. Let's say you have an idea or your friends say you should do something, like with Adam, the Texting Prince. Ask, "How much would you pay me for my technique?" They might say $19 or $99. Start with that.

Another good tip is to go through Amazon, YouTube, and Facebook and find out what others are teaching and how much they are charging for it. You might not charge the same amount, especially since you are new on the scene, but it will give you an idea.

You will have to keep testing your prices over time, gauge your audience, and adjust as you go. Always expect to change your price. Sometimes you will ask for too little. Sometimes you will want to improve the product and ask for more later. If you improve the value you are delivering, you should charge more.

## GUIDING QUESTIONS

Now that you've read a bit about product development, here are a few guiding questions to consider as you develop your product.

- Who is your audience? Start with yourself. What did you think about when you were in your customer's situation or experiencing their pain at the beginning of your journey?

- Is there a critical mass to support your product? If so, how do you find and interact with them? Are they part of your tribe? What do they need? Are there business owners who could benefit from and pay for your expertise?

- Can you imagine a product you could create based on your expertise? Can you further tailor or narrow your product to meet specific needs?

- Have you ever bought a book, digital content, or a course online? How much have you spent on it? Can you improve it or add your unique personality and knowledge to it?

- Have you ever asked friends or family how much they would pay you for what you have?

# CHAPTER TEN

# TAKE FLIGHT

As I mentioned in Chapter One, the word *Kajabi* means to take flight.

I first heard this word at the summer camp I worked at while in college. I didn't know what it meant, but I loved the sound of it, and the way it rolled off your tongue: Ka-ja-bi. I loved the word so much that I bought the domain Kajabi. com, although I didn't do anything with it for years.

When Kenny and I were thinking of names for our software platform, we threw out a bunch of possibilities. I already owned the domain Kajabi.com, so we just went with it. It wasn't until we started to brand and market ourselves that we found out the real meaning behind the word. It was like it was destiny. The meaning of *Kajabi* fit perfectly with what we were trying to achieve.

There's an important truth here: in a lot of your journey, you're not going to know what you're doing, but if you just take the chance and go for it, I promise you big things are going to happen. Do you remember when I said that, somehow, all the dots will eventually connect? This was one of those moments.

*Kajabi* is an old aboriginal word, meaning flight. To them, a bird's flight probably looked like a miracle. Then, when they first saw a plane in the sky, they also used the word *Kajabi* to describe the flight of that plane. We all take for granted the idea that we can just hop on a plane and fly to the other side of the world, but if you stop to think about, it's truly a miracle. I mean, you're in a big tin rocket-like thing with wings that don't flap, all weighed down with luggage and people, and somehow it just flies.

That is like the journey you are about to go on. You hear me talking about something you haven't yet witnessed firsthand. You haven't experienced it, but it can happen. Just like people doubted that airplanes would ever fly. It looked impossible at first, but now thousands of people use planes to fly around the world daily.

As you'll recall, Kajabi's mascot is a duck, and a duckling's first flight is a guaranteed failure. The mama duck pushes the duckling out of the nest, and he always falls to the ground. I'm sure it hurts when he hits the earth, and I'm sure it seems impossible for him to fly at first. Through trial and error, though, the duckling finally flies.

I tell you this because I want you to know that you will probably undergo a similar process. When you first start building your knowledge business, I'm sure you will have some failures. It's never easy, and most Kajabi customers I've talked to have had all sorts of beginner struggles. It might be difficult at first, but I promise you, *you* can do this. Especially if you think in your head right now that you can do this, then you really need to go for it.

So just get up and take your first flight. This chapter is going to show you what to do from here on out. I want you to think positively as you move forward. Start imagining yourself doing this and going for it.

## STARTING YOUR YOU, INC. BUSINESS

First, it's important to realize that you already have everything you need to start your business. You have already gained expert knowledge from your real life and your real experiences. You don't need to get a degree, special training, receive a license, or get a certificate.

Look, if you are one or two steps ahead of those you lead, you're still leading. So often, we say, "I can't do this until I'm there," or "I can't do this until I'm perfect." But the reality of life is that the person who just stands up and leads is the leader. It doesn't mean you have to say, "I'm an expert at everything. I've done everything." If anything, your real struggle and empathy for others will be better for leading than your perfect life. Be yourself. This will attract your tribe, your audience, the people who will feel most connected with you. People will love the authentic you.

You have all the equipment you need, so there are no excuses. People always ask me, "What do I need to get started?" You have a phone, right? Unless you're still rocking a Motorola pager, you probably have a phone with a camera on it. That phone is enough to take a video and post it. Most of you probably also have a computer. If so, you literally have everything you need to launch this business right now.

## LAPS

I'm going to now take you through a series of steps that I call LAPs. I call these steps LAPs because I picture this process like you're running a race. If you're starting a race and know there are three laps, you can't just skip the first couple laps and jump to the finish line suddenly. The first lap is just as important as the second and last lap. This is a journey, and what you learn along the way, how you fail, how you keep going, and how you try new things will give you more confidence later.

## FIRST LAP

What is the first LAP? This is where you begin to take flight. This is the first stage of your journey.

Imagine yourself sitting on a plane. The flight attendant has announced imminent takeoff, and the plane begins to move. It starts to shake, tremble in some places, and it's kind of scary. This is always when my wife literally grabs my hand and clenches it. But once the plane takes off, you're flying, and you stop thinking about how the plane is actually doing it. You might even forget that you're in the air. You might fall asleep or watch a movie. But the takeoff itself always seems scary and sometimes impossible. That's when you should commit and just go for it.

I want to warn you again about speaking to friends or family too early in your journey because, most of the time, they might discourage you. They might say, "What makes you an expert? Why would anybody want to listen to you? Why would anybody pay you money?" In your first LAP you really want to avoid that kind of feedback. Imagine you are starting your race and the people on the sidelines are telling you, "You will never finish. You can't run. You suck." How will this help you complete your race? It won't. So be careful with who you let stand on your sidelines. Anyone that says your idea is not worthwhile should not be invited on your journey.

You must truly believe in yourself when you start. If you have people around you who are positive and believe in you, certainly share your vision with them. But negative people will be like anchors on your plane. It will never take off, and if it does somehow take off, it will be messy. So remove all the anchors right now. No matter what, please make sure you choose wisely who you involve in your journey.

Let's now go through what is involved in the first LAP.

### First L: Landing Page

A landing page is a web page that has information on it which encourages potential customers to reach out for more information. For example: "Hey, I have the solution for you to this problem. I have already gone through this, and I'm going to give you the information you're looking for." Someone reads the landing page and gives you their email address. Then you provide the information to them by email or via downloadable link.

Your landing page is your first introduction. It's kind of like walking into a store, and the salesperson says, "Hi, welcome to Apple. My name is Jeremy. Can I help you?" The only difference is you are meeting someone through the internet. To connect with them, you will transfer value to them, and the value you're giving is knowledge—the beginning of your knowledge. What you give them could be all kinds of things, but what you get in return is a way to contact them: their email.

This is the beginning of the journey: a landing page.

There are a few key elements your landing page needs to include. The first is a clear statement about who you are. This doesn't mean a bio. It means a clear description of how you are going to help the reader. Maybe you are a nutrition specialist or a dating expert.

Right underneath that, you want to describe what you're offering. For example, what is the change or benefit the potential customer might gain? A big point to know about online marketing is that features don't mean anything. It's all about benefits. People are asking, "How is this going to benefit me?" If you think of all the stories I shared, each person offered a benefit to others. Every one of them focused on the change or outcome. Start with that.

A couple examples of benefit or outcome are these: "You're going to lose ten pounds. You're going to fix your credit." Again, start with the outcome within the niche you are focusing on. Discuss what they are getting: relief, assistance, a solution, a new skill, tips and tricks, etc.

Focus on sharing what you have discovered about your

niche and what you can offer your audience. This is important because some of you have discovered a solution that the customer doesn't know about yet. They only know about their problem. For example, if you are talking about intermittent fasting, you wouldn't necessarily want to start there. Instead, talk about the problem of fatigue, weight gain, or menopause as a woman. Talk about the struggle so you can then explain the solution and benefit.

The next thing you can do is include a video of yourself, only if you feel comfortable doing so. You don't have to do a video, but I highly recommend including one because you will connect with more people that way. It doesn't need to be perfectly professional. If you are your raw self, willing to share your flaws, mistakes, and all your imperfections, that is the best way to gain connection. Nobody wants fake people solving their problems. Inauthentic people make customers feel uncomfortable, like they might be selling snake oil. You don't want to be that person.

### First A: Awareness

A in the first LAP stands for developing awareness among your potential customers, among your tribe and the people you are going to connect with.

You need to go out and spread the word. Keep it simple: Facebook or Instagram. Pick one, or pick both, but don't do anything else right now. You don't want to get over-whelmed. On Facebook or Instagram, you are going to talk about your niche. You are going to share your solution and your hacks. You're going to identify other problems in the space, but first talk about your problem and how you solved it.

This is how you are going to turn your online presence into a brand. Sometimes we use the word *platform* interchange-ably with brand. We say, "This is your platform." People might say Tim Ferriss or Gary Vaynerchuk have platforms. They're known based on who they are. Oprah is a perfect example of one of the most powerful personal platforms. This is what you're doing too. Usually, the brand is built around you as a person. Be your true, authentic self. Trust me, this works wonders.

As you build this, reference all facets of your life. Every-thing. Talk about the mistakes or whatever else. For example, my wife was doing a podcast the other day, and she mumbled her words in the middle of it. She left her mistake in there, and I said, "That's kind of cool you did that." My wife is a smart woman, and she knows her stuff. Sometimes she messes up; it's what makes her human, and it's why people connect with her. Do things like that. It's very important to be yourself. Don't fix all your mistakes.

You may want to use another identity. You might not be

Oprah or Gary Vaynerchuk, but you might be the "Yoga Queen." If that is the brand you have worked on, and you know it works with your customers, you can use that. Just be you, all of you, whatever is behind that name. It's fine if people use that name to refer to you and remember you, but make sure they know all of you. You are not a mascot for a sports team inside a costume. Your costume is yourself.

People need to know you and trust you. Once they do, they will open their minds and hearts to whatever you're sharing, and it will start changing their lives. Knowledge is about warmth and connection. Information is just cold and impersonal. I can find information right now. I can Google things and read things. But knowledge is a real person connecting to me and helping me. That's where the real power is.

### First P: Basic Product

The P in the first LAP stands for the first basic product you will create.

Remember that on the landing page, you are offering something to visitors that they can download. It must be something of value for them to be enticed, and it's best if that downloadable thing is free. Yes, free. You might be thinking, "If I give away information for free, why would anybody ever pay for it?" I get this question a lot.

When a potential customer can download that first basic product, they start to trust you. They see you're trying to help them and realize you're not just in this for money. You'll find that later you can charge for an entire course on the same subject. Even if you have given parts of the course away for free before, you'd be surprised how many people are still willing to pay for the whole thing because it's curated and perfect.

Compare that with others online who say they will give you something, but then demand payment first. If this is your first time "meeting" that person you might be taken aback. Why should you trust them?

You've probably had the experience of trying something for free and thinking, "Wow, that was awesome. I want more, and I will pay for it." That's what you want to do here for others. Think of the yogurt shop. You look at all the flavors and think, "Oh, I think I want that kind of yogurt," but you're not sure and can't make up your mind. Then they hand you a small cup with a free sample, and then you say, "Okay, I'm totally getting that." You are doing the same thing here.

Give your visitors something to come back for. Actually, give them the best stuff. The yogurt shop doesn't say, "Well, I will give you a sample, but it's missing the sugar or the toppings." Don't try to hold back the best stuff. Give them the best so they'll want more of it.

That is how you leverage reciprocity. When you give to people, people will give back to you. It's the law of giving, and it works every time. You give out something for free, and in return, you're collecting email addresses. This allows you to start building your email list and interacting with potential customers.

This is a great example of the old business versus new business difference. In an old business, you would hand out a business card or brochure or send newsletters, hoping that someone stumbles across your ad and follows up. In the new business, your product is at their fingertips and immediately benefits your customer. You give them something of value, and they can learn something right away. They think, "Wow, that worked. I want more of it." In the new business, people are expecting to receive the benefits immediately, rather than just hear about them.

### THE HUNDRED-DOLLAR HUSTLE

Remember Dr. V, the bariatric surgeon from Chapter Five? He's an active doctor and very busy. He had an idea to make videos to help patients after surgery, but he procrastinated for months. Finally, he created five simple videos, which he sold for just ten dollars. As soon as he finished and offered the videos, he made a couple thousand dollars in the first couple weeks just with an initial basic product.

I'm going to challenge you right now to do something I call the "Hundred-Dollar Hustle." Here's what it is: you create one simple product that you will sell for ten dollars. All you have to do is sell this product ten times, and you will make your first hundred dollars. Don't procrastinate. Just do it now. Maybe you'll fail, but who cares? You might be surprised by what happens. Start now; take flight on your journey.

## SECOND LAP

What comes next? As you know, once your plane takes off and the shaking and rumbling stops, you start to feel more relaxed, but your journey is really just beginning. On your second LAP is where you're out there offering products. The real products, the ones people will pay you for.

It's important to note here: you can stay in the first LAP as long as you need to. You could do multiple lap ones. Maybe do it for a while as you're building a customer list and gaining confidence. You want to make sure you have really developed the awareness among your end users by doing the first LAP for a while. There is no set schedule when you should finish the first LAP. Eventually, when you feel confident in your product, it will be time to move on.

Remember the story of Jordan, from Hardcore Music Studios, who gave away the drum files. He gave those files away for a long time to build his list. When he was ready to start selling products, he had a list of people ready to go.

### Second L: An Improved Landing Page

L in the second LAP again stands for landing page, but this is a much more developed landing page, designed to sell your product. At this point, you will know more about your customer's needs and wants, and this new and improved landing page can have testimonials, new information, and videos.

You may even have a full-fledged website at this point. But be sure to keep your original landing page up, the one from your first LAP, because you can use it to keep collecting emails. Dr. V talked about how he kept the original landing page up and how it continues to bring in a couple thousand dollars here and there on autopilot.

### Second A: Audience

The next part is to grow a real audience. You've been creating awareness on social media. You've been making posts, and these posts don't just say, "Buy my stuff. Buy my stuff." They tell people about your journey. You're helping people. You're fixing things. You're encouraging others and giving them amazing solutions. It's important to not just sell to your audience. You need to continue to talk about the subject and connect with them. Share tips, hacks, quotes, blog posts, or videos. Allow them to see and connect with the real you.

You're creating your tribe. This is the group of people that have the same interest and are looking to you as a leader. Once you start building your tribe, you can talk to them. It's important to interact with this audience as much as you can. You might give them some direct requests for their input about what they want to learn, and they will give you valuable information, and soon you can survey them. You'll realize, "Wow, they all want to know this." You might end up making a product you would have never known anybody wanted or needed.

This way, you will have some real value to offer others. This way, you will grow your audience through word of mouth. This is how things become viral. Why does something become viral? Because it's amazing. It's funny. It had an effect you didn't expect. Maybe it solved a problem you had never heard of before.

So start sharing your amazing journey. And don't just share the amazing parts, think about the hard parts of your journey, the struggles and the failures. Share all of it. Help others. People will relate to you when you do this, and soon, an audience will grow.

*Second P: Product for a Price*

The P in this second LAP is about offering a more valuable product—one you can charge money for.

On the first LAP, the product may have been free, but this time around, there's a price. Now that you have developed a connection with your customers and they trust you, they will be willing to buy from you. In fact, they may even be telling you, "Hey, you should make a course on that."

Remember the Texting Prince, whose buddies were constantly asking for help with their dating lives? He helped them for free repeatedly, and eventually his friends were like, "You should charge for this." This happens all the time. If you help people, they're going to want to pay you money. Give yourself permission to charge and make money.

When you know what your customers want, build a course around that. You can help them grow. You're not just blindly throwing out responses based on what you read in a book. You're talking about your journey—how you found what you needed and how they can too.

Elissa, the voice coach, learned everything she could, and then she coached others. They would ask more questions, and she would spend months learning so she could return with more answers. This is important. You've been called to lead these people, so take it seriously. Don't just throw any old info back to them. Figure it out. Try it for yourself. Make sure it works and say, "Here's what I tried. Here's what happened." That kind of leadership works every day.

Another great example is Tamsen from Chapter Six. She began teaching via Skype. She didn't have a plan. She just took what she knew and connected with her audience—stay-at-home moms who needed trademarking and attorney services. She would reach out to them and say, "Hey, I can help you with that." And she did it in her kitchen, at her house, right where she was. Sometimes you would even see one of her kids sitting on her lap. She didn't try to make it perfect. She just reached out, offered something of value, and charged them a little bit of money. Then she started growing her audience of moms and entrepreneurs and eventually developed an online course just so she could continue to connect with more people.

Her example shows how things can become easier as you go. An airplane can't stay on the runway the whole time. A plane can't fly until it takes off. The first part of flight seems scary and difficult. An enormous amount of thrust is needed to get the plane and passengers off the ground. The important thing is to not stay in the difficult area if you don't have to. As soon as you can start automating and working smarter through something like an online course, it's time to do that.

Now you're on the final lap. You're ready to reach new heights. This is the part of the flight when you're at cruising altitude. You can take your seatbelt off, order a cocktail, and enjoy the flight. I say this because it's time to relax. But you also must finish the journey. It's not like you can stay up there forever having drinks with your feet up. This is what a lot of people do once they get to this point, but the most successful knowledge entrepreneurs keep going and coordinate a launch.

### Third L: Launch

The L in the final LAP is to create a launch. A launch is a time-based event in which you target all your customers using the email list you've already created.

This launch event will have a buildup: for example, you will send an email to your customers that you are launching a new product, course, or book and that they will be the first to get it. You can even put a set date and limit the amount of access. This creates scarcity, and people love to be the first to something new. Think about how Apple does this with their new iPhones. People stand in lines for hours, sometimes even camp out, just to get the new iPhone. To get the excitement going for your new product, you will have to release a series of emails.

There are many ways to create a launch. I am going to give you a very basic and general guide to doing a launch. It's just a simple example, and I want to encourage you to learn more about how to do a product launch. For more in-depth examples, I highly recommend checking out Jeff Walker's Product Launch Formula on jeffwalker.com.

Here is my basic example of a launch.

The first email needs to be personal and conversational. The goal of this first email is to get your customer to open it and read it as if you had sent a personal message directly to them. In this email, you will identify a problem that you have experienced. For example, you can ask them if they are in deep credit card debt or if they've had problems losing weight. The email must show empathy and extend a real human connection, telling the customer who is reading the email that you have been down that road too and that you have discovered a solution. At the end of this email, there should be a call to action link. This email should entice the customer to learn more about your journey through this problem so that they opt in to be a part of this launch.

Not everyone from your original customer list will hit the call-to-action link and opt in. Don't be discouraged. In time, you will learn how to improve your copywriting skills. Remember, it's not about being perfect; it's about being your true self. If you want to improve your click-through rate, meaning you want more of your original customers to join your launches, work on your copywriting skills. Look up Frank Kern. He is the best at email copywriting and teaches you how to find your voice and improve your conversion rate.

The second email is sent on a later date. It's typically one or two days after the first email or sometimes the next week, but you don't want to take too long in sending the second email. These emails are usually staggered in a certain time frame. Again, look up Jeff Walker for more advice on this. In this email, you start talking about the possibilities of life beyond the problem you described in the first email. You can talk about how great life is now that you've solved this problem. Remember, the goal is to keep them wanting more. For example, let's say your business tackles debt. You would say how wonderful it is to have an 820 credit score. How stress free it is to not have creditors call your house at all hours of the night. In the case of losing weight, how nice it is to fit into your high school jeans again or how fun it is to have all this new energy from losing all that weight.

This email also needs to have a call to action that leads the customer to want to hear more about your success stories. You can even post a video of yourself and maybe other customer testimonials. Videos work wonders; they are the proof that you are genuine. People love to connect and see the face behind the words.

The third email sent will identify the path. For most of you, it's the path you took to solve the problem. You are starting to show the customer how you will get them to the same goal. You will show them how simple it was for you and how easy it can be for them. There will be another call to action where they can find some components to your course. For example, you could give them a budget worksheet or a tip on how to rotate their credit cards. You could give them exercise tips or protein shake recipes. You are giving them a taste of what's inside your course.

The last email in the sequence, the one we have been building up to, is called the pitch. This is where you enthusiastically tell your customer about your product, book, or course. This is where you get them to sign up and pay you. You have already described the problem, life beyond the problem, success stories, and shown them a small portion of the path you want to take them on. This is where you invite them to join you. By this time, your customer can't wait to go down that path with you. They can't wait to sign up. A good way to get them to sign up is to let them know the course will only be available for a limited amount of time or for a limited amount of people. Basically, it should say, "Here it is. Here is the price. Buy today, or you will miss the boat!"

I want to be very clear: this is just a quick example of how a launch works. There are a ton of ways to do it, so please do your research and use what works for you and your tribe.

A lot of people fear new launches, but those who are willing to do a launch are the ones with the biggest success stories. I saw this firsthand when we launched Kajabi. It took us almost a year to build a sellable version of Kajabi. During that year, we were building our list, our first customers were testing it out, and they were having huge success. On the bottom of all their landing pages was a link to Kajabi. That link led back to us. People signed up and wanted to be the first to try Kajabi out when it launched. Our list grew and grew, and they literally couldn't wait for us to launch. As we got closer to the launch date, we started sending out the emails, like I mentioned above, to build the anticipation. By the time we launched, people were begging to sign up.

Think about that for a second. Remember the Hundred-Dollar Hustle with a product that costs only ten dollars. What if you had a product worth $1,000? There is a customer on Kajabi who teaches you how to become a best seller, and she charges $10,000 for one course. I know that sounds like a crazy amount to charge, but her customers' success rate is in the 90 percent range, so you get what you pay for. A high-end product must deliver. If somebody signs up for your big product and you charge a lot of money, you will be held accountable. It's a lot more hands-on.

You might end up charging a lot of money for your big product because it's worth it. And if it's worth it, people will pay for it. If it's not worth it, they will let you know. At the same time, if you're going to go big, don't get discouraged. If you can envision it, you can achieve it, but you have to believe in it.

### Third A: Authority

A in the final and third LAP stands for authority. So far, we have talked about awareness and audience. Now you need to have authority. This isn't about ego or becoming the perfect leader for your group. It's about having influence. Now the opportunities come to you. You may even have to turn down some of those opportunities. This might be crazy to think about, especially considering how much you might have struggled in the beginning. If you haven't started yet and the airplane is still on the runway, this can be especially crazy to think about.

But once the airplane is in the air, you can put the airplane on autopilot, just like pilots do. They set it for the course, and it goes there. I'm not saying you will put the plane on complete autopilot, but you will find ways to get to your destination more quickly. It might be crazy to think about. But the work will be fun, energizing, and enjoyable.

Once you have authority, you could start speaking at events. You may write a book, like I've done, or maybe the major companies will contact you, like they did with the Sugar Mama. She is now an authority in sugaring, and major companies send her customers because her online training is more accessible than any in-person training. Shannon has a constant flow of customers at this point because of her authority.

### Third P: The Ultimate Product

This P is what I like to call the ultimate product—the mastermind. A lot of people try to start here, which is why their journey is so difficult. Don't even touch this until you have done the first and second LAPs. I'm only telling you this P so you can look ahead and start to dream about it.

A mastermind is where you can move beyond a product and hold an event—either online or in person. Even if it's only ten people, those people will come and spend the day or weekend with you to learn from you and share experiences. Think about it as an accountability group where all of you talk about the same topic, discuss the same goal, or go through the same course with you as their guide or leader.

The value you would get from a mastermind is huge. The energy you get from the people, and the information and feedback you receive, is more valuable than the money you can make from holding such an event. Not only are they going to learn from you, but they also learn from each other, which can make your tribe more connected and allow your message and movement to grow beyond you.

The concept of a mastermind was coined by Napoleon Hill, the author of *Think and Grow Rich* and *The Law of Success*. There are different variations of how masterminds are held. You can do these masterminds in person or virtually via video chats. Masterminds typically meet once a year, once a month, or even once a week.

The reason why masterminds are the ultimate product is because people are willing to pay thousands of dollars to attend such events. Think of Tony Robbins. His events bring in thousands of people because they want the experience. An event like his is immersive. People get to meet other people on the same journey and end up creating a bond with each other that is exponentially powerful.

If you get to this P, your tribe will want access to you personally and will pay to see you live. The sky is the limit. Remember, the reason why you should do your first and second LAPs is because you need to build your audience, you need to get their trust, and you also need to refine and perfect your voice in your knowledge niche.

At this point, don't get discouraged when we talk about money. You may still be a bit skeptical about what to charge or what people are willing to pay. Maybe you are still questioning yourself and wondering whether you really are an expert. Trust me, once you have done your first and second LAP and have gained the trust of your audience and seen what people are willing to pay for your course, you will start to gain the confidence you need to get through your third LAP.

## YOUR GPS-DRIVEN JOURNEY

The best advice I can give you is to have patience. When you decide to go on this journey, you must remember it won't always be a flawless take off. You can input your destination into the GPS system, but you need to trust it and go for it. I always had a vision for something better than working out of a cubicle. I knew that I didn't want to work for someone else for the rest of my life. I knew I wanted to become an entrepreneur. I just didn't know how it was going to come together.

Remember that GPS stands for God Pushing Softly.

If you're quiet enough and trust enough and believe in

your destination, you'll know what to do next. I know you have heard that voice before, the one that tells you, "Hey, you are really good at this," or "Wow, you really can help people because you have been there too," or "Man, everyone should know about this," or "Someone should do something about that." That someone could be you.

Twenty years ago, when I first started meeting up with Kenny for lunch, we would bounce all sorts of ideas around. We had no real concept of what was going to come from our early meetings. But we both were positive that we could come up with something great, and we just kept moving forward. I wish I could tell you that Kajabi was our first idea and it exploded, but that is not usually how it works. We explored all kinds of ideas. Some failed, some are still brewing behind the scenes, but after many years, one finally took flight.

And if you mess up, don't worry about it. God or the voice you believe in—maybe the Universe—will tell you what to do next. I promise that you will fall and fail a couple of times before you get it right. If you want to get mad, get mad, get upset, cry it out, but then, when you are done having your fit, meditate, journal, pray, and get quiet, because soon the GPS will say, "Recalculating your route." Listen, you may take the wrong turn, but it's okay. You can always course correct. Just get back on course and keep heading toward your destination.

## THE HERO'S JOURNEY

If you've ever watched movies like *Star Wars* or *The Lord of the Rings* or even *Frozen*, then you've seen the Hero's Journey. The hero is usually inconceivable and very reluctant, but they hear the voice, and they are being called to do something great. They must leave the known and head into the unknown to achieve this great thing. As the hero travels to this unknown place, there will be problems, obstacles, and even antagonists trying to stop them. Watch out, because some of those antagonists are usually the people closest to the hero. Throughout the journey, the hero also meets mentors, guides, or maybe a sidekick who helps the hero get to their destination. The hero will often be tempted to quit and go back to the known because that's where it's safe and comfortable, but these helpers will keep the hero going.

The protagonist in this Hero's Journey is *you*. Many people just like you have heard the calling, met problem after problem, met antagonist after antagonist, and failed more than once. But those heroes also made course corrections and continued their journey and did something great. That's part of the Hero's Journey. It can't be a Hero's Journey if you don't get out of the known. So move out of your comfort zone and step into your greatness.

Listen, I will be the first to tell you. No one gets it right the first time. Here I am writing a freaking book. Me, a kid who stuttered until he was eighteen. A kid who got bad grades. A kid whose teachers would tell his mom that he wouldn't amount to much. A kid who flunked out of college. Everyone who knows me personally, knows that my biggest insecurity is writing. I hate it. I hate it so much that when I send a text to anyone, I usually double- and triple-check what I write and then rewrite it, sometimes not even sending the text at all for fear that people will criticize my writing.

People in my inner circle didn't even think I could start the process of writing a book, much less actually finish it. But I knew that I had to share this knowledge. I knew that people needed to hear the stories of my customers. Along my Hero's Journey, people have mocked me and my ideas. I've been criticized, put down, and laughed at. Imagine if I allowed their voices to be bigger than the voice inside of me. I would have stayed in that windowless cubicle, never allowing my ideas to see past the pages of my journal.

I love the story of the Hero's Journey, and it's an idea we use a lot at Kajabi. In fact, we call our customers who have made their first $1,000 in sales "Kajabi Heroes." The reason they are heroes is because they left the known, went to the unknown, and came back to share their knowledge with the world. They became the mentor, leader, or guide and helped others go through the same Hero's Journey.

Now, I know some of you have already gone through such a journey. The powerful thing about heroes is that you tend to go on multiple journeys throughout your life. Look, life isn't about learning just one thing and stopping. It's about constantly evolving, learning, and growing and using your newfound knowledge to teach and help others. That is the beauty of You, Inc. You don't have to stop at just one unique niche.

Now you can go through the process we have talked about in this book. You can help others on their journeys, which is the heart of You, Inc. It's about going through your journey and listening to your inner voice. Most people ignore it. But if you're reading this book, that means you're going to do something. You, Inc. is going to change your life, your family's lives, and the lives of everybody you touch along the way.

Don't try to advance through these LAPs too quickly or skip a stage. It's all about incremental forward progress. Seeking to share your purpose to benefit others is truly heroic, and it betters your life too. You have heard my story, my journey of stuttering and struggling in school. To this day, I still freak out when I get in front of a camera or in front of an audience because the fear of my stuttering is always in the back of my mind, but I do it anyway because I know how important it is.

I have accomplished some of the greatest things when

I've gotten past my fears. When you focus on helping others, you will have success. That's what heroes do: they help others regardless of the obstacles and fears. Once you stop complaining about your situation and recognize that what you went through has a purpose or a meaning, you'll be a hero before you know it.

I have said this before, but I'll say it again. The struggles and challenges you have gone through were not for nothing. You went through them so that you could help someone else. That is the essence of the Hero's Journey. So many people could benefit from you putting your knowledge out there.

That airplane is on the runway, but the view from the air is so much more magnificent. You won't be able see the city lights or the ocean or the snow-topped mountains unless you take off. You must take off. It's scary, but who cares how scary it is? The view is worth it.

# CONCLUSION

What is the future of knowledge capital? It's the democratization of knowledge, with average people becoming experts, sharing knowledge, and building businesses in areas they never may have considered otherwise.

The internet started with information, but knowledge is about people. I call it the human knowledge network. It's people in the world connecting with other people. Ultimately, I believe it's what God intended.

There are billions of little nodes of information inside the human brain—more than the stars in the universe. When a network across the internet works, it's connecting one computer to another computer to another computer. The more it connects, the more powerful it becomes.

This is the human knowledge network. This is what happens. This is what the internet has caused. Kajabi has been able to become a powerful source for people to reach out and help other people, helping people connect with more people to become a stronger human network.

## JOIN THE MOVEMENT

This is a movement, and if you're reading this far into the book, it means you're now part of it.

I know there is something inside of you that you can share with the world. Sharing your knowledge can enable you to change your life and the lives of others. I always think back to when I was in a cubicle. My whole life, I looked forward to the day I didn't have to work on my parents' farm under the hot sun, and I couldn't wait to get a high-paying job in an air-conditioned office. When I finally got there, my only thought was, "Wait, this is it?" I couldn't believe that was all the corporate world could offer me. Eight- to ten-hour days, one-hour lunches, two fifteen-minute breaks, two-week vacations max, and if you were lucky, three days of sick leave. Oh, and let's not forget the Monday morning commute and the Friday evening traffic jam home. Really?

I had all these great ideas, and my creativity felt trapped inside me. I knew I had to break free from that cubicle life and share my knowledge with the world. The same is true for you. There is something else you are supposed to be doing, and you need to do it. Your destiny has already been set; just follow the GPS and see where it takes you.

## YOU ARE A BUSINESS

Business is not something external; it's something inside of you. Look out the window and see where you are. For so long in my life, I kept my head down and just worked hard. That's what I had learned from my parents. *Work hard. Work hard. Work hard.* But if you do that all the time and never look up, how will you know if you are heading in the wrong direction? What if this whole time, you have been working hard to get somewhere you don't want to be? What if you are wasting your gift and talents to make someone else more successful?

You can leverage the experience in your life right now. Where have you been? What have you overcome? Who can you help? And where do you want to go? The journey is not always smooth. Often, there are obstacles and challenges along the way. The first step can be especially challenging, and then that is followed by incremental steps forward. I talked about the plane on the runway. The plane cannot take off until you're ready. So make sure you're buckled up, trust the process, and fly.

Start the journey, and see where it takes you.

## TAKE THE FIRST STEP

I really want to help you get started on this journey. Go to YouIncBook.com for additional guides and resources to help you along your journey. I also love to hear success stories, so please send me yours once your plane takes off.

# APPENDIX

- Jon Acampora—excelcampus.com

- Garrett J. White—warriorweek.com

- Scott Perry—scottperrymusician.mykajabi.com

- Nicole Begley—nicolebegleyphotography.com

- Diane Bleck—doodleinstitute.mykajabi.com

- Remi Boudreau—expressionspaintinguniversity.com

- Matt Codde—ocdacademy.com

- Shane Dowd—GotRom.com

- Jermaine Griggs—hearandplay.com

- Tamsen Horton—tamsenhorton.com

- Adam Jordan—textingprince.com

- Keith Kalfas—keith-kalfas.mykajabi.com

- Jeanne Kelly—jeannekelly.net

- Leah McHenry—savvymusicianacademy.com

- Shannon O'Brien—isugaruniversity.com

- Dy Ann Parham—dyannparham.com

- Michelle Parsley—elevateyourart.com

- Felicia Ricci—feliciaricci.com

- Zach Spuckler—heartsoulhustle.com

- Jordan Valeriote—hardcoremusicstudio.com

- Dr. Duc Vuong—DucVuong.com

- Elissa Weinzimmer—voicebodyconnection.com

- Kendra Wright—heykendra.com

# ACKNOWLEDGMENTS

First, I need to thank God. As a little farm boy that stuttered badly, I prayed to God to show me something more, to help me and change my situation. He did just that and has taken me on a wild journey. Sure, there have been many ups and a lot of downs, but regardless of it all, I'm grateful that God had a plan bigger than I could ever imagine. I am so thankful that I heard His voice, followed it, and faced my fears.

Throughout this process, my wife, Paola Rosser, has been my rock. She encouraged me when I wanted to quit, she was there when I needed help, and it's only because of her that I had the courage to write and finish this book. I'm so grateful God gave me a second chance and sent me someone as amazing as her to spend the rest of my life with.

Next, my parents, Jerry and Carolyn Rosser. Growing up wasn't easy, but my parents always loved me, supported my crazy dreams, did the best they could, and served as a good example.

My business partner, Kenny Reuter, who helped me cofound Kajabi. We've been friends for over twenty years and I wouldn't have been able to do this without him.

Andy Jenkins, who was our first Kajabi customer and helped us get the ball rolling. Thank you for taking a chance on Kenny and me.

Jermaine Griggs, who planted the seed for Kajabi with his inspirational life story.

Garrett J. White, thank you for pushing me to write this book.

Thank you to the Kajabi team. I can't thank you guys enough for all your hard work.

Finally, a great big thank-you to all Kajabi customers. Your stories continue to inspire me all the time.

# ABOUT THE AUTHOR

 TRAVIS ROSSER is an internet entrepreneur, author, speaker and software designer. After a decade in the software industry he cofounded Kajabi, a knowledge capital platform that has helped customers redefine themselves as experts, free themselves from the traditional notions of a job, and live more fulfilled lives. Since 2010, Kajabi customers have generated over $500 million in sales, and Kajabi has helped more than 10,000 people become knowledge entrepreneurs.

To learn more about Travis, you can find him at:

www.TravisRosser.com